Sixteen Years in Care

David Meader

malcolm down

PUBLISHING

Copyright © David Meader
First published 2022 by Malcolm Down Publishing Ltd
www.malcolmdown.co.uk

25 24 23 22   7 6 5 4 3 2 1

The right of David Meader to be identified as the author of this
work has been asserted by him in accordance with the Copyright,
Designs and Patents Act 1988.

British Library Cataloguing in Publication Data
A catalogue record for this book is available from the British Library.

ISBN 978-1-915046-33-8

Cover design by John Tromans

Printed in the UK

Foreword

*'Blessed is the man whose strength is in you,
whose heart is set on pilgrimage. As they go
through the valley of weeping, they use it as a
well . . . They go from strength to strength.'*

(Psalm 84:5-7)

My wife and I met David and his wife Else at the church
in Dulwich that David mentions in chapter 30 of this book.
We became friends and have remained in touch through
their subsequent adventures both at home and oversees.
As David mentions, we have worked with him for many
years on a course which we run, and which is a little like
the Wholeness Through Christ course that was so helpful
to David.

As a former psychiatrist – now long retired – I have always
been interested in how people can change over long
periods of time. The changes that David describes in his
book are truly remarkable. David's childhood was marked
by an almost complete deprivation of any contact with any
member of his family. He lived in a children's home with
over 200 other children and during the holidays he was
often the only child who stayed on at what was called 'the
Homes'. The other children went back to their families

but for David this was not possible. Yet no one who meets him today would realise any of this. Today he is a warm, intelligent and humble man with a salty wit that contains perhaps a residue of past pain. How is such change possible?

In his book David describes the importance to him of three foster parents at the Homes and the principal whom he describes as his advocate. Judging by his recorded behaviour at the Homes, which sometimes involved fire, David needed a good advocate! He needed people who would believe in him. He says little about the four of them, but he dedicates the book to them and later in the book he mentions how, years later, they all came to his wedding. The goodness that David received from those fine people must surely have given him a basis for hope which held him together through some truly dreadful times.

The turning point of the book came in the period after leaving the Homes. At this very low point in David's life, he discovered that God loved him. Fortunately for us, David kept a diary of what followed and much of the remainder of the book is illustrated by quotations from that diary. The diary contains the daily thoughts, prayers and Bible readings through which he was gradually able to make sense of his past, to chart a course through many difficult situations and to find God's plan for his future. The book will be an inspiration to many and is the sort of book that one can read and re-read and find new gems with each reading.

Stuart Checkley
Psychiatrist and Professor (retired)

Acknowledgements

I would like to thank all those who have over the years encouraged me to write this story. They are too many to name individually, but you know who you are! My wife Else has been a constant source of encouragement and constructive criticism ever since I first started writing in earnest. Our good friend Phil Davison sacrificed a great deal of his time in the midst of other pressing demands with the Summer Institute of Linguistics to edit and improve the first and considerably longer draft. My former boss Trevor Matthews made self-employment possible so that I was able to write as and when I needed to. And my friends Marilyn and Stuart Checkley have given me countless opportunities to tell my story to others during Transformed Lives sessions over the past twenty years. Without you, this book would not have been possible. Thank you!

Preface

This book is about my childhood, 16 years of which were spent in care. For much of my early adult life I wrestled with the consequences of that childhood. Those who looked after me during those years were kind, committed and caring, and I will always be grateful to them for choosing a vocation that must at times have seemed both challenging and thankless. The quality of their care for me was exemplary. But most of all, they kept me safe. Certainly safer than any of the alternatives. So, this is not a book about child abuse suffered at the hands of paedophiles and predators who infiltrated state-run care settings at that time; but rather, a story of how my intense feelings of rejection, pain and loneliness often resulted in periods of deep introspection, unhelpful internal dialogue and occasional outbursts of anger that left me confused and bewildered. How I came through this struggle is related in the story before you, and the fact that I did is a tribute to those who cared for me during my childhood.

It is also a tribute to those who continued to love and support me after I left care and struggled so much to make my way in the wider world. That period forms the second part of my story and takes me into my early 30s.

As you read on, you will discover that a childhood spent in care does not have to lead to underachievement and a lifetime of unresolved pain. Difficulties and pain there were. But I hope that you will conclude that these can be overcome.

My story is especially for those of us who have lost all hope that our circumstances can change, or that we can recover a sense of self-worth and purpose. For those who struggle with uncontrollable feelings of rejection and anger; for those who feel abandoned and confused; for those who feel unable to trust others and despise themselves for their failings. And for those of us who have been wounded and have erected defences to protect ourselves from ever being hurt again, while at the same time realising that those very defences rob us of the intimacy and freedom from fear that we desperately crave.

We are all in some sense 'broken', and like china plates that shatter on the floor we all break in different ways. This means that some aspects of my story will resonate with you while others will not. I hope and pray that those parts of my story that touch you will also help you. You will be introduced to other broken individuals dealing with their pain. Most have made significant progress on the journey to restoration and wholeness; others have not.

My restoration and renewal could never have come about without some key relationships. I eventually felt safe enough in those relationships to be honest about just how much I was struggling to hold it all together, to finally put my pride aside and to admit that I had run out of ideas and desperately needed help. It was unconditional love that helped me face my pain and forgive those who had wounded me so deeply. This was the key to my gradual restoration and to a life with purpose.

In what follows I mention many who have played a part in making my life what it is today. But special mention must go to my carers and my teachers.

My carers include Mr and Mrs Addison who took me in when my young mother was in such desperate need. Miss Potter, Miss Val Chivers and Miss Miriam Cambridge who so lovingly cared for me during my pre-school years. Miss Mary Thomas who looked after me aged three and a half to seven during a time of great personal distress. Mike and June Shearn who took me on during the most formative and challenging years of my childhood aged seven to seventeen. Mr John Honey who succeeded the Addisons as principal was my advocate when I had no one else to turn to. And there is also Mrs Winnie Miles, whose genuine concern and sacrificial generosity lifted a very heavy burden from my young shoulders.

My first teacher at pre-school was Miss Burleigh, who gave me my first lessons in life. My teachers at Park Lane Primary School include: Mrs Ecclestone, who taught me the basics of reading and writing; Mr Dewdney, who instilled discipline; and Mr Ord, who made learning such fun. At King Ethelbert Secondary School my thanks go to Miss Pither and Mr Sullivan for having faith in me; to Mr

Marshall for making English so interesting; to Mr Morgan for giving me a love of history; to Mr Tuppen for making me see sense; and to Mr Teasdale for taking my aspirations seriously. At Dane Court Technical High (now Grammar) School my thanks go to Mr Drake, the headmaster, for providing a place at his school, and to his staff, for taking me to the next level. My thanks also go to my lecturers at the former 'Butts' Technical College in Coventry who accompanied me during some of my worst trials, and to Dr Christine Bellamy at Trent Polytechnic (now Nottingham Trent University) for seeing my potential.

Each of these people trigger such positive memories in me, and in looking back on those years I am filled with a sense of gratitude and thankfulness. But it is especially to Mary, Mike, June and John that I dedicate this book, with a full heart and grateful thanks.

Author's notes

I have changed some names and locations to conceal the identities of some individuals. The words in italics are usually quotes from my care records and my diaries. In other places italics are used for emphasis.

The proceeds from the sale of this book will be donated to the continuing charitable work of the Spurgeon's Children's Charity.

Contents

Chapter 1

Perhaps You Remember Me...

'Perhaps you remember me...
I am in trouble once again.'

It was my mother who was in trouble. These are the opening lines of her letter to Mr and Mrs Addison, the principal and matron of Spurgeon's Children's Home. The date was 24th August 1961 and my mother, Virginia, was then 22 years old, and I was not yet two.

There was no 'perhaps' about it. The Addisons remembered my mother because she had been in their care for part of her own troubled childhood. The letter describes her *difficulties*. She meant by this that she was an unmarried mother living in sub-standard temporary accommodation in Kilburn, north-west London, and was *desperate to get David settled and also to find work*. She asked that I be admitted within seven days and on 31st August I became Admission No. 4635. I was to stay at Spurgeon's for the next 16 years. During those years I never once saw my father; I saw my mother very intermittently and my relatives even less.

At its peak, 'the Homes' (as it was known locally) cared for up to 240 children who, like me, had been placed there either by their parents or by the statutory social services. The Homes was located in the village of Birchington-on-Sea in the county of Kent. Set out in over 30 acres, the site comprised a large hall for babies and toddlers, and three blocks of four houses for school-age children. Each house catered for up to 18 children under the care of two house-parents and a relief house-parent. The cooking, cleaning and gardening were undertaken by a band of paid locals who came in faithfully each day. Others such as the quartermaster, the ladies who did needlework repairs and some office workers lived on-site in separate accommodation, as did the relief house-parents and those caring for babies and pre-schoolers. I therefore shared my new home with over 200 children and 60 or so adults at any one time. It was very different from being raised by a mum and dad!

During my time in care I experienced more loss and change than the average child of my age. There was the constant loss of childhood friends and caring adults who left the Homes for good. This was because children typically stayed at the Homes for maybe three or four years before returning to a parent or relative. The Homes generally accepted children below the age of ten, meaning that when I reached the age of ten there were far fewer children of similar age. During the long summer holidays, I was frequently the only child of my age who stayed at the Homes for the full six or so weeks. I must have cut a lonely figure; I certainly *felt* lonely. So, although I was not alone, companionship came at the price of bereavement as I formed close childhood relationships that were bound to end after three or four years. I was also an only child. And, of course, I did not have the permanent parents that most children took for granted. In fact, I had several parent substitutes.

So, it will not be surprising that loneliness often features in my story. Some of us find it possible to be alone without feeling lonely; others can be surrounded by people and yet feel incredibly lonely. Maybe this is because we feel different, that we simply don't or can't fit in. For me, it was also the physical loneliness: the holidays with no one to play with within the vast sprawling emptiness of 30 acres in which I served my sentence, hour by solitary hour. I therefore had plenty of time to dwell on that recurring unanswered and unanswerable question: 'Where *are* my parents?'

Separation, pain, loss, loneliness . . . Eventually feelings of rejection followed. Initially these feelings were kept at bay by the genuine love and care I received from my carers. But they could not compensate for what only my family could provide. They could not take me on holidays when all the other children went home and returned with smiles on their faces and carrying new toys, clothes and shoes in bright new shopping bags. Why couldn't I, like them, go home during the holidays? My carers couldn't give me those special presents that only a mum and dad can give – those labelled with the precious words I so longed to read: 'To David, love Mummy and Daddy xxx'. The house-parents tried their best to compensate a little for what was lacking, but both they and I knew it was not the same. Despite all their efforts, I nonetheless felt increasingly different from my companions and increasingly let down by my parents. Feelings of rejection emerged amid a host of unanswered and unanswerable questions: 'Why am I different? What have I done to deserve this? Have I done something wrong?' And 'Do any of my relatives really care?'

I was constantly trying to make sense of my situation, especially when in my view other children were getting a better deal. They went on holidays with their parents; they received better Christmas and birthday presents than me; their parents wrote to them and visited them more regularly than mine did. The conclusion I drew from these observations was that I didn't deserve these things. So I felt rejected: somehow I wasn't worth the effort. That conclusion was difficult to accept but seemed to be the only sensible answer to the equally painful question, 'Why me?' Nor could I find a satisfactory answer to the related question, 'Why am I here anyway?'

Chapter 2

Questions and Answers

It was when I began primary school just before my fifth birthday that I first started to ask earnestly, 'Why am I here?' At this stage this wasn't the existential question about my life's purpose: that would come later. Right then, I felt a deep need to know why I was in the Homes while other children at my state school lived with their parents.

All I knew was that up to this point my whole life had been lived within the confines of the Homes. Yes, I had lived my first 21 months outside the Homes, but I had no conscious memory of that time.

The Homes met every practical need. I was being given three meals a day, and I was being washed, dressed and put to bed with the spaces in between filled with play at nursery school. I have very fond memories of my pre-school years at the Homes, so I had little cause to question why I was there. My pre-school world is dominated by four ladies. First was the matron in overall charge of babies and pre-schoolers. She was always known as 'Miss Potter' and her deputy, Miriam Cambridge was known to us pre-schoolers as 'Auntie Miriam'. These two and another lady, Val Chivers, looked after me in what was referred to as 'the Hall'. This was the former Birchington Hall, a stately home dating from the 16th century. It was located well away from the three blocks of 12 houses where the school-age children lived, and was adjacent to a purpose-built nursery and pre-school building complete with sandpit, swings and other outdoor pre-schooler delights.

Mrs Burleigh was in charge of the pre-school. She was always referred to as such and, like Miss Potter, was a kindly lady in her 50s who never seemed to age. Mrs Burleigh would stand no nonsense from us and would firmly reprimand any of the 12 or so children under her care who got up to mischief. But her favoured approach was to keep us physically active, encourage our creative talents and to offer boiled sweets as reward for good behaviour. My pre-school days were days of wonder. I was experiencing so many things for the first time. And I was just old enough to possess a sense of wonder about the world in which I lived and to appreciate the beauty and awesomeness of this world I had been born into.

Some of my most vivid memories at that time are of the beauty of the dazzling blue sky, the white purity of the clouds, the whispering leaves in the swaying trees and the sweet smell of freshly cut grass. At times it was a totally immersive sensory experience. I would enter a timeless world as I gazed skyward, fascinated by the gentle forming and reforming pure white clouds against the brilliant blue sky. Apparently, the house-parents would see me doing this as I made my way home for lunch and puzzle over what I was doing, standing with my feet glued to the path with my neck right back gazing upwards. As I made my way home from pre-school I enjoyed leaning lazily against the old oaks and elms, running my hands slowly over the textured bark while thoroughly absorbed by the variegated colour of the leaves. On gusty spring days I stood mesmerised as the larger trees wrestled with the winds, their huge boughs lumbering majestically up and down and side to side. The stars at night were another great source of wonder to me. Sometimes, when I could not sleep or in the early winter evenings when night fell so quickly, I would draw the curtains aside to leave a head-sized centre gap, press my nose against the cold glass and stand fascinated at the twinkling dots of light against the black sky. All this was new, it was exciting, and it made me feel good to be alive. And one incident stands out amongst them all.

I remember being four years old at the time and standing on the path on my way home to lunch from pre-school. I had reached what was known by everyone as 'the hole in the wall'. (You can just about see it just over halfway up at the left edge of the photo with a path passing through it leading west on the other side of the 'hole'.) This separated the blocks of houses from the area occupied by the Hall, pre-school, sick bay (a small health centre with children's wards) and Principal's house. I had always been fascinated by the ever-changing patterns of the clouds against the crystal-clear blue sky and the way that the trees and the flowers and the grass all seemed to be part of a seamless pageantry of colour and of life, death and new life. On this occasion, I was simply awestruck by the sheer immensity and beauty of it all. It was all so much bigger than me and made me feel incredibly small by comparison. These natural rhythms seemed to have a life of their own that continued whether I was present or not. But somehow, I felt as if I had been invited to be part of it and I happily immersed myself in it all, looking up and letting the whole spectacle enfold me and carry me wherever it would lead. That incident was, in retrospect, quasi-spiritual. Of course, I could not put it in those terms at the time. For me, this was not Nature communing with me but rather me sensing that there was a Presence beyond and an 'Other' quite apart from Nature: a sense that this beautiful world was created by something or someone quite different from Nature itself. I had been told by my carers that that 'someone' was God. This experience left me with a sense that God really did exist and that this was his awe-inspiring world. This encounter is the earliest memory I have of trying to answer the question that I was then far too young to put into words: 'Who created this world in which I live and where did it all come from?'

But by the time I reached primary school age a few months later, such questions were completely overshadowed by my need to know why I was in a children's home and yet most children at school were not. Of course, that inevitably prompted a closely related question: 'Where are my parents?' This was particularly pertinent because I was becoming aware that most children were cared for by their parents and not simply *house-parents* as I was. There were also other differences between those of us from the Home and the other children, such as the clothes they got to wear, the food they were allowed to eat, the pocket money they were given, the time they went to bed . . . The list was endless, and the grass looked distinctly greener on their side of the pasture!

Primary school was therefore the catalyst for a host of questions. I couldn't know at the time that, as a matter of policy the principal and the matron gave the house-parents very little information about why each child was in care. So, whenever I asked why I was at the Home I was told that my mother was too ill to look after me and that my father lived in another country. These answers were factually correct but completely unsatisfying. After all, I reasoned, people who got ill also got better, didn't they? But she never seemed to get better and so that explanation didn't make sense to me. More than this the house-parents were unable to say, and perhaps that saved them from having to answer what were unanswerable questions, or from saying something which would be more unhelpful than helpful to the children.

All I knew as I began my first year at primary school was that there were two groups of children: those who grew up with their parents and lived at home and those of us who were 'from the Homes'. This phrase 'from the Homes' recurred throughout my time in care. During both primary and secondary school, a child was categorised as either 'from the Homes' or not. At least, this was how it seemed to me. This distinction was further reinforced by the clothes we wore and the standardised short-back-and-sides haircuts we were given. Over the years and as fashion changed, the haircuts remained the same. At primary school, the boys from the Homes all wore grey shirts, green-striped ties, short black trousers, grey socks and the clunky black shoes which as teenagers we disparagingly called 'beetle crushers'. We were very distinctive.

Girls from the Homes all wore the same uniform although hairstyles were more varied, from the single ponytail, through double bunches, to well-brushed freestyle.

The sense of 'us and them' was further reinforced by the way we travelled to school *en masse*. The green-and-grey army of Spurgeon's children wended its way from the Homes to Park Lane where the school lollipop man shepherded us across the road through the school entrance twice each day. The whole effect was that we children dominated the route to school and could be clearly identified by our attire and hairstyles as being 'from the Homes'.

What also distinguished us from other children was that it was virtually impossible to cultivate normal relationships with children outside the Homes because of the care model then in place. This was brought home to me when I was invited by a classmate – Robert – to his birthday party. I was probably eight at the time as my house-parents were then Mr and Mrs Shearn ('Uncle Michael' and 'Auntie June'). I can't remember how I got to Robert's house, but I do remember being mortified to find that I was the only child who had not brought a present. It was humiliating to stand in the queue with the other children and, on reaching Robert, having to apologise for not having brought him a present. Even if I had known that bringing a present was expected, my pocket money was completely insufficient for something acceptable, and I did not have parents to help me out or tell me what was required. I was not invited again, and for that I was glad. I had felt so embarrassingly different. Another thing that struck me at Robert's party was how relatively wealthy his parents were compared to the children I knew so well who lived on the route to school. Robert's parents lived in a nice part of Birchington in a detached property near the sea, a fair distance from the Homes and from my council estate friends. Robert's house featured comfortable furniture, plush carpets, and spacious rooms; his parents appeared well spoken and well presented in clothes that I had never seen before. From this point on I started to notice such things: what people wore, how they spoke, how much pocket money they received, what toys they had, where they went on holiday and what kind of houses they lived in.

I was also introduced to the world of professions. Parents at Park Lane School were predominantly working-class, with a smattering of managers, shopkeepers and owners of small businesses. One boy particularly intrigued me. His name was Nigel. He fascinated me because he was the only boy in the school who sported a gold tooth. Was this, I wondered, the mark of a truly wealthy child – a gold tooth? Nigel soon left our school for something he called a 'private school'. The rest of us were none the wiser. But his departure did get me wondering why some children were at Park Lane and others attended 'private' schools. It also made me reflect on where I featured in the pecking order. I concluded that although there were definite disadvantages to being from 'the Homes', there were also advantages. These were most evident in the routines and rules we were expected to follow.

Chapter 3

School Day Routines

A typical school day would start at 6:40 am when one of the house-parents called us to get up, get washed, get dressed and make our beds. There were two bathrooms in each house – one for each gender – and the 16 of us children vied for the use of the two toilets and six sinks available to us. Chores started at 7:05 and included cleaning, dusting, sweeping and polishing duties. There were yards and yards of dado rail and skirting board to dust, many square yards of tiled floors to sweep, and lots of taps and mirrors to polish and sinks and toilets to clean. The fact of the matter was, we children occupied a large living area. Upstairs there was one large bedroom consisting of six beds, one medium bedroom with five beds and three small bedrooms with two beds each and two bathrooms (plus a staff bathroom). These upstairs facilities were all connected by very long corridors with a wide and shallow 22-step staircase leading to the ground floor. Downstairs were two cloakrooms, the playroom, the staff sitting room, the utility room and the children's sitting room. The dining room lay off a long corridor leading to the huge, centralised kitchen. All of these were cleaned by the children each day, although some of the more difficult duties, such as washing and polishing the floors, were performed by a paid cleaner. So, chores were part of my life from an early age, and they taught me the importance of regular cleaning and maintenance. We had to repeat chores that were sub-standard and this repetition typically took place during breakfast time. This meant that the offending child had less time to eat breakfast than the others and would probably feel hungry during the morning while at school.

Breakfast began at 7:40 sharp but was preceded by a mandatory 20-minute Quiet Time when the house-parents gathered us in the main sitting room to listen to a passage from the Bible. They then gave a brief homily, and we said some prayers. This reflected the origin of the Homes as a Christian charity founded in 1867 by the renowned Victorian preacher C.H. Spurgeon. The site in Park Road was its third location since being established as the Stockwell Orphanage in south London. The Quiet Times were variable in terms of instruction and enjoyment, depending on what passage was read and which house-parent led proceedings. All staff were expected to be committed Christians, but there were noticeable differences in understanding and practice. Nonetheless, to most of us the Quiet Time represented our main contact with matters spiritual and religious, and it certainly imbued in me a deep awareness of the omnipresence and holiness of God. He, it seemed, was everywhere and expected good behaviour from me. Because of that I much preferred Jesus, who seemed to be more approachable, child-friendly and understanding, although I didn't quite understand how Jesus and God were related.

The meals at the Homes were a highlight. The food was plentiful, and we were encouraged to eat heartily. Waste was strictly prohibited, and we were expected to eat every morsel even if it took more than one mealtime to complete the task. I often had to eat my unfinished fish and chips from lunch time for tea – sometimes with a bonus portion added for good measure! I tried all sorts of strategies to complete the meal including administering copious amounts of vinegar and salt to disguise the flavour and gulping down a mouthful of water to drown each tiny morsel. Any attempt to smuggle unwanted food out of the dining room in pockets, hands or under the guise of needing to visit the cloakroom was a high-risk strategy, and usually unsuccessful due to the uncanny vigilance of the house-parents.

On one occasion when the unfinished fish came back at teatime with an additional cold portion, and I had been left to eat it alone, I tried another tactic. The house I was living in (Barrington) was adjacent to a house called Waterbeach. The Barrington dining room overlooked the Waterbeach courtyard, and as I peered through the window I spied Tom, the Waterbeach cat. The solution was obvious – give the cat the fish to eat! There would be no tell-tale evidence and the cat certainly wouldn't tell. So I opened the window and called the cat over. It didn't move, but I was so desperate that I tossed the vinegar-soaked fish several feet out of the window towards the waiting feline. The cat took just one cursory sniff to decide against eating my offering and disappeared out of sight. I was dumbfounded and started to panic. I knew full well that I couldn't just leave the offending item in the courtyard for the Waterbeach house-parents to find. They would soon put two and two together and it would not be long before I would be facing a very severe punishment. So I had no choice but to climb out of the window and creep unnoticed across the courtyard to retrieve the rejected item. I struggled to clamber back in without being detected but I made it. However, I now had a piece of food that even the cat wouldn't eat – and was now peppered with grit and dirt. I spent the rest of the evening prodding the fish with my fork and praying that the house-parents would relent and not expect me to eat it for breakfast. My prayers were *not* answered: it duly appeared the following morning. Just the thought of eating it made me want to gag and I had to leave it again. Mercifully, it did not reappear for lunch – probably because it had become a health hazard. But all morning while at school I had been dreading that I would be forced to eat both it and another bonus portion at lunchtime. Such was the seriousness with which the Homes took any needless waste of food.

Breakfast was always three courses: cereal (porridge in winter), a cooked course and bread or toast and marmalade, all washed down with generous amounts of copper-coloured tea dispensed from large (later small) steel teapots. The teapots were so large and heavy that it was not until I was at secondary school that I had the strength to lift a full one and pour a steady cup without injuring my wrist or pouring the tea in a wild, uncontrolled semicircle across the tablecloth.

The cooked course at breakfast was quite often fried bacon rashers, baked beans and exquisitely deep-fried golden bread triangles. We children loved this food and occasionally it was possible to obtain *third* helpings, especially if one or more children had to repeat chores during breakfast. Their loss was our gain, although they were always given cereal and bread and marmalade as a minimum. However, there was no guarantee that there would be sufficient second helpings for every child. So, each of us developed various strategies for getting through the cereal phase and first helping as speedily and as surreptitiously as possible. This was necessary because the house-parents were frequently on the alert for children who tried to reduce their cereal intake in order to obtain pole position in the queue for second helpings of the cooked food. It has to be said that the cereals (unlike the glutinous sweet porridge) – cornflakes and Rice Krispies – were not filling, and if one missed fried seconds then one had to compensate with at least three slices of white bread or toast if one was to avoid mid-morning hunger pangs at school. None of us had the money to buy additional supplies from the school tuck shop to tide us over, so an effective breakfast strategy was essential.

Breakfast, as with all meals, commenced with grace – thanks to God for our food and remembering those children who didn't have enough. At times this was said with a heavy heart and inward groan when the food before us was not to our liking.

Breakfast was usually over by 8:10 at the latest and then we embarked on the second round of chores. These were all laid out on a rota. In total, each child was expected to complete as many as 40 chores each week. Although this was hard work, we soon realised that the best approach was to accept that there was no escape and get it over and done with as quickly as possible. It was an inconvenient but unavoidable fact of life at the Homes, and it reduced cleaning costs considerably.

All of us returned to the Homes for lunch each day: there was just enough time to walk home, eat lunch, complete our chores and return to school. Most of the other children at school ate school dinners, either out of convenience or because they were poor enough to qualify for free school meals. So lunch was another event that differentiated us from the others. The main disadvantage was that we missed out on school lunchtime games and being with our friends. The great advantage, though, was the quality and quantity of our meals. I once stayed for a school dinner out of interest and wished I hadn't! The portions were small, insipid, and satisfied neither the palate nor the stomach. Overall, then, we felt the advantages outweighed the disadvantages.

The school day ended at 3:25pm and we had some time to ourselves before tea at 4:10, at which time the secondary school children joined us since they finished school 20 minutes later. We primary schoolers used the time before tea to polish and shine our shoes or, in summer, our sandals. The secondary schoolers cleaned their shoes after they had completed their teatime chores, and free time (after chores of course) began as early as 4:30.

The evenings were always a highlight for me. When the weather was inclement, we either played together in the large playroom or sat in the children's sitting room and watched the limited children's programming on the black-and-white TV. But even when colour TV arrived, we tended to limit our viewing to the specific programmes we liked, such as *Doctor Who*, *Star Trek* and *The Sweeney*. This was because the two alternatives to TV were so overwhelmingly attractive. To be honest, we were spoilt for choice: do we play in the spacious well-equipped playroom located at the end of each house, or outside on the well-equipped playground?

Sport was something that the Homes positively encouraged and, apart from its generally acknowledged benefits, was one of the main ways we developed a strong sense of camaraderie and solidarity. We dominated the school sports teams and for us, sport held out endless options to succeed. In addition to a variety of sports equipment, the purpose-built pavilion at the Homes also housed rows upon rows of team photos of football, cricket and netball teams from times past. I can still remember some names of the team members. Two things struck me as I perused these black-and-white photos on the walls: first the photos showed the physical growth of individual children over the years. So, I could, for example, see how one youngster in one team photo developed with every passing year. The second striking feature was how many of the teams featured children from the same family. I found it interesting to match the physical features of the siblings with their surnames as I passed along the rows of framed photos. To me this was merely an interesting exercise, but in reality this sporting prowess hid family tragedy and breakdown.

On any fine evening it was not uncommon to witness two games of football being played on the large playing field. These would start at around 5pm and morphed into a structured game any time after that as children finished their chores and joined in greater numbers. There was at least one game comprised mainly of the older boys (usually the 11+ age group) and sometimes a smaller and rather chaotic game comprising primary aged boys. The girls confined themselves to activities on the playground which had been extensively redesigned and renovated when the new Baby Hall was built in 1967. The favoured location for the older boys' pitch was in the corner bordering the tennis courts and a strip of land commonly called 'the bushes' that separated the playing field from a farmer's field. The pitch covered an area of about 40m by 20m although the touchline opposite the bushes tended to set itself. The goals were defined by a pile of sweaters and the centre kick-off spot by approximation. We self-refereed the match with respect to fouls, penalties and whether a goal had been scored. This was made easier because we did not play the offside rule and any 'goal hangers' who might take advantage of this were rarely rewarded by their teammates who did the hard work of tackling, defending and dribbling.

Team captains were usually the most skilled of the older boys, and they chose their teams by selecting individuals alternately from an initial pool of about 12. The sides were gradually enlarged by others who joined having completed their early evening chores, and each side often had the benefit of a male house-parent. There was, for example, the giraffe-like bespectacled John Stevens (Westwood house in Block 1) with his distinctive ginger hair and enormous Adam's apple. John packed a kick so powerful that any child foolish enough not to dive for cover was likely to get hit and leap around frantically rubbing their searingly painful thigh (as I often did). John would let fly whenever the goalposts seemed remotely within range and would regularly cut a swathe through any kind of defence we children could muster. The other regular footballing house-parent was David Alexander (St David's house in Block 2): he, by contrast, tended to dribble around players rather than scything his way through them. David passed the ball to us much more than John did, and so some boys preferred to be on his team. The downside to this meant you were subject to John's cannonballs. We eventually worked out a strategy for neutralising the 'Stevens Cannonball' by sending in a couple of younger boys to nip at his ankles before he could get up momentum. If John had been a less caring person he would have trampled over the children, but he was a house-parent after all and didn't want to be responsible for injuring children a fraction of his size!

The end of the game was determined either by fading light or the gradually diminishing number of players as they set off for bed from around 7pm. It was not unusual for some games to continue until 8pm, but most of us wanted to eat some supper and watch a little TV before bedtime, so numbers started to diminish significantly after 7pm and the game would draw to a natural close.

The bedtimes were set according to age as prescribed by government-decreed Home Office regulations. None of us children knew what the 'Home Office' was, but it was clearly something that could not be challenged. The easiest way for us to remember bedtimes was the 7/7 rule. This meant that a seven-year-old had to be in bed by 7pm. This increased by 15 minutes for every additional year. So, a nine-year-old would be in bed by 7:30pm and a six-year-old by 6:45pm. This was increased by 30 minutes on Friday and Saturday nights because of the weekend, and we were given a 30-minute lie-in on Saturday and Sunday mornings. This meant that a 16-year-old could stay up until 9:15pm on most days and until 9:45 at weekends. At what time we actually fell asleep was an entirely different matter. We got up to plenty of pranks and, from time to time, had our backsides warmed with a slipper!

The pre-bedtime routine was fairly constant. Each child was expected to have a strip wash or a bath before settling down for the evening. Baths were always on Tuesdays, Thursdays and Saturdays. 'Correct' washing was ensured by inspection of our ears (inside and behind) and our hands before we moved on to our 'smalls' (underwear and socks): these also had to be presented for inspection. Once that chore was completed it was time for us to settle down to some TV and then, for the younger children, a story from a house-parent.

Some of my fondest memories as a young child are of bedtime stories being read by my favourite house-parent Mary Thomas. Miss Mary, as she was known, was in her mid-20s, of moderate build, with black hair and piercing blue eyes. She was probably the same age as my mother and so an ideal substitute. She was one of several women who had a strong positive influence during my early years. Miss Mary cared for me from the age of three and a half to the age of eight.

As young children we were all bundled off into the bath two by two to save time and water. Some of these bath times are captured on a promotional film commissioned while I was at The Dingle (Miss Mary's house), and they capture the fun of these occasions during our early years. I can still remember the bath bubbles, the smell of the Swan soap and the soothing talcum powder as we were towelled dry and dressed in our bedclothes for story time. Usually, the story was read to us as a group of maybe four to six children in Miss Mary's sitting room. Occasionally, Miss Mary would read after we were tucked up in our beds. The pre-bedtime routine was a pleasurable and calming one, and we always finished the day with prayers for our parents and other loved ones. I would usually fall asleep soon after. If I had difficulty getting to sleep then Miss Mary would wind up my white clockwork musical poodle with its nodding fluffy head and wagging tail and set it plinking away to the tune of 'Little Donkey'. I was usually well away before the clockwork mechanism had completely wound down.

Occasionally the poodle was unable to work its magic and I simply could not sleep. So I adopted another technique which was to focus on the flower patterns in the bedroom curtains. This was only possible during the lighter evenings because the light had to pass through the curtain fabric to illuminate the flowers printed on the material. My great favourites were roses that were duplicated at regular intervals across the fabric. I found that by concentrating my gaze on any of them, individual petals would come to life. I would lie there mesmerised by the lifelike detail of the rose and the gentle toing and froing of the curtain as it was wafted by the cool evening breeze. Before long and quite imperceptibly I would drift into a deep and restful sleep.

Chapter 4

Weekends

Chores had to be performed on the weekends, of course, but Saturday and Sunday activities were very different to weekdays. Saturdays were usually visiting days. We did not know at the time that our parents were required to visit us every two weeks as part of their agreement with the Homes. Most parents had to travel long distances, typically arriving at the Homes late in the morning and returning their children in the evening or sometimes the next day (although this was rare). Other parents, my mother among them, arrived after lunch and returned their children after teatime.

This meant that there were insufficient numbers to form football teams on Saturdays, so we would pursue hobbies indoors. This was the time when we tended to play games with those in our own house, often facilitated by the house-parents. There was plenty of scope for cooperation but also for competition and conflict! During inclement weather and the holidays, we were expected to entertain ourselves.

I don't remember much about Saturday mornings during my days in the Dingle except that it was the opportunity to spend my pocket money at the Homes' tuck shop. This was provided on site especially for children under 10 years of age, since they were not permitted to venture beyond the Homes to the local shops unless accompanied by an adult. Pocket money was administered according to age: I think I started with 3d per week when I arrived at The Dingle as a three and a half-year-old and finished with 50p a week by the time I left Barrington at age 16. My abiding memory is having just enough money to buy a large bottle of R White's lemonade, cherryade or orangeade and a packet of sweets. One of the regular 'dares' was to insert a sugary Love Heart sweet into the fizzy drink bottle and watch the chemical reaction produce a short-lived but spectacular jet of bubbles and froth which shot out of the narrow bottleneck. It was great fun watching it, but it was inevitably followed by a sense that maybe drinking it would have been better than wasting it in order to amuse others. There were lots of alternatives to the 'R White's drinks and sugary sweets' combination, and all of us sought to obtain the maximum number of sweets for our money. These included four-for-a-penny chews such as Blackjacks and Fruit Salad, sherbet Dip Dabs, solid yellow and red sherbet lollies, Cadbury's chocolate, and Mars bars (which we were convinced really did enable us to work, rest and play, as the advertising slogan so persuasively suggested). There was also the inevitable post-tuck-shop bartering when we exchanged sweets between ourselves. Regardless of what we bought, tuck shop was a greatly anticipated high point of the week. Other Saturday morning activities were variable, and we were very much left to our own devices unless an adult organised an activity. In The Dingle the options were to play in the playroom or in the private courtyard, a paved area with a large circular flowerbed and a small lawn cordoned off by a low wooden fence. My favourite activity was splashing in the inflatable paddling pool on sunny days.

Activities for the older children of Barrington House were much more varied and exciting because Uncle Michael often joined in, playing board games, table tennis and snooker with us. He also helped us with model making and took the lead in constructing an extensive small-gauge railway complete with tunnels, realistic landscaping and rolling stock. Ensuring that the multiple trains did not collide with each other was almost as exciting as driving the Formula 1 Scalextric cars. These got so much use that their wire contact brushes needed replacing very regularly, and they would frequently grind to a smouldering halt mid-race having been denied time to cool down. One of the great advantages of being in a children's home was that we were often given lots of second-hand toys, such as the Scalextric and railway tracks. With these we could construct long and challenging circuits that other children could only dream of. These games worked well during term time but when I was on my own during the holidays these activities only served to remind me just how alone I felt. It was no fun playing on my own, so I often resorted to reading assiduously or playing chess games from books as these activities passed the time most quickly.

Occasionally, Uncle Michael would introduce a completely new activity or challenge. One of the most memorable of these was produced by an electronic device that he constructed. It consisted of a solenoid which could be calibrated from low to high power. We were required to hold in one hand a metal tube which was connected to the device while another metal tube connection was placed in a bucket of water. The device contracted our hand muscles, and the challenge was to thrust a hand into a bucket of water to grasp a 50 pence coin placed at the bottom before our fingers contracted into a curl. I'm not quite sure how it worked but it was great fun, despite being quite painful. But we were always up for the challenge, even though I can't remember any of us breaking through the pain barrier to grasp the elusive prized coin. So there was usually plenty to do indoors on Saturday morning in addition to any outdoor activities.

Saturday afternoons tended to be a lot quieter, not least because many children would be out with their parents. Those of us who were ten or older were permitted to walk into Birchington or even to the seaside resort of Margate, although this was a six-mile round trip. So those of us with no visitors would typically stay in the Homes and find things to do which didn't require the presence of other children. Two of my favourite hobbies were model making and stamp collecting, but I also watched TV or simply pottered.

During the summer, we were often taken to the seaside on sunny Saturday afternoons. This involved either walking the one and a half miles to Minnis Bay two by two in crocodile fashion or travelling in one of the two minibuses. We usually arrived soon after lunch and it was, like the tuck shop, something we all looked forward to. Minnis Bay was the nearest beach that was safe and enjoyable for children. The Homes had a beach hut on the promenade which provided the luxury of hot drinks and limited shelter from inclement weather should we need it. It had a distinctive beach-hut smell – a mixture of slightly damp wood, sun cream and sea salt – and was equipped with a portable gas stove, deckchairs, spades, buckets and windbreaks. When the tide was out, we camped on the sandy beach and spent most of our time splashing each other and paddling in the warm shallow water and then building grand sandcastles with huge retaining walls and deep moats to defend against the incoming tide. The climax of the day was frantically coordinated activity to reinforce the retaining walls and to build up the main sandcastle. We knew that the walls and castle would eventually succumb, but it was great fun to see how long we could hold out.

Once changed out of our costumes we settled down to a picnic tea in a substantial grassed area called 'The Dip' which was set well back from the concrete promenade. The tea typically consisted of Sunblest white-bread sandwiches with a variety of fillings: grated cheese, chocolate spread, sandwich spread, meat or fish paste, jams of various types or peanut butter. We ate these voraciously and quickly drained our disposable plastic Kia-ora orange drink cartons. We bolted down anything else that was offered – cake, cheese portions in foil wrappers, scotch eggs, beetroot, apples, pears or oranges ... In order to maximise the options for football, rounders and other team games, it was quite usual for several houses to visit Minnis Bay together, so we had no problem forming teams and thoroughly enjoying ourselves.

In contrast to the walk *to* the beach, which was conducted in an excited and energetic manner, much more effort was required to complete the homeward journey. On arriving back at the Homes, sand was quickly shaken from clothes and between toes and each child sped through the usual ablutions before falling soundly asleep soon after.

Sunday was very different from the other days. The early morning and the mealtime routines were the same, but the focus of Sunday activities was completely different. It was a special day of rest in accordance with the Home's conservative Christian view of the Sabbath. This view changed in the 1970s with the retirement of Mr and Mrs Addison. The new principal, Mr John Honey, persuaded the Trustees to allow a wider range of activities. But in my early years the conservative view prevailed.

Following breakfast chores, we were each required to write a letter to our parents, whether they had written to us or not. My mother wrote sporadically, and what she did write was of little interest to me unless it promised a visit or a present of some kind. Writing to my mother became a burdensome and largely pointless duty. My letters were stereotypical, short and usually devoid of substantial content. A typical letter would run something like: *'Dear Mum, I hope you are well. I am. This week I did X, Y and Z. I hope to see you soon. Love David xx.'* My mother's letters also tended to be predictable. It was as if we were two people trying to communicate through a thick soundproof glass sheet. The externals of communication – the words and formalities – were present, but there was no real engagement. So for me, letter writing was just another chore – something to be got out of the way as quickly as possible. Not that there was much to look forward to on Sunday mornings. We were not permitted to play outdoor games of any kind, and instead were encouraged to read or to play card and board games.

But we were required to attend services at local churches in the morning and a shorter service at the large modern chapel within the grounds during the evening. At 10:10am we were dressed in our Sunday best ready for the march to Birchington Baptist Church. Some old-school house-parents insisted that the boys be doused with hair grease known as Brylcreem for that extra smart look. Brylcreem advertisements portrayed male models coiffured to produce what was called 'the Brylcreem bounce'. This was all well and good when the Brylcreem was judiciously applied – one large sachet typically lasting a whole week. This point was completely lost on some who vigorously adopted what can only be called a saturation policy, meaning that not one hair was out of place, but also that on some days the grease melted and found its way down the back and sides of the boys' collars. Not so much a Brylcreem bounce; more a Brylcreem slick! I managed to escape that greasy ritual apart from the odd occasion and I can clearly recollect the unpleasant sensation of the cold oily white mass being squeezed out of its sachet and slapped on my head as I moved towards the cloakroom to massage in the unwelcome anointing.

We marched to our respective churches in pairs with one house-parent at the front and the other at the rear to supervise us crossing roads and to ensure that we made way for pedestrians walking in the opposite direction on the narrow paths. The simplest route was to turn right out of the main gate until we reached the main road. There we turned left towards the village square with its solitary roundabout, parish church and clusters of ancient pubs and modern shop fronts.

The square was dominated by the towering flint construction known as All Saints Church which was famous for being the resting place of Gabriel Dante Rossetti, a leading figure in the late Victorian Pre-Raphaelite arts movement. The remaining buildings were long-standing public houses such as the Powell Arms (named after the owners of the local Quex Park estate) and the Queen's Head. This was the era when shops were closed on Sundays except for newsagents, guesthouses and hotels.

Eventually the unexceptional line of modern shop fronts the other side of the roundabout was interrupted by a distinctive large corner shop called 'Barrows', situated at the corner of Crescent Road. The proprietor, Mr Barrows, was the exclusive supplier of shoes to the Homes. This was not a cause for rejoicing since the only shoes we were offered were, in our considered opinion, styled with a complete lack of imagination and were mocked by our school friends. The shoes were functional and good value for money but, like the Spurgeon's dress code in general, were a constant source of embarrassment to us.

The dress code, like our haircuts, illustrated two fundamental tensions between what the Homes needed and what we children wanted. For the Homes, it was important to reduce costs and to treat each child equally. The bulk-buying of standard goods such as shirts, dresses, underwear and trousers achieved these goals, as did standardised medical check-ups and haircuts. As for us, we wanted to be treated as individuals and have a choice like our school friends. We grudgingly learnt to live with this tension, but we never accepted it. It was part of the price of living at the Homes.

So, on Sundays we dutifully trooped off to church, wearing our standard clothes and standard shoes and sporting our standard haircuts. Passing Barrows and turning right up Crescent Road we soon arrived and filed into the Baptist church vestibule just before the appointed start time of 10:30.

Chapter 5

God and Religion

The Homes' policy was to send each child to their parents'
preferred denomination, but logistically it made sense to
send the whole house to just one local church. In my case
this meant Birchington Baptist church. Others were sent as
far east as Margate to either Cecil Square Baptist (which
had an exciting balcony) or the Salvation Army citadel with
its brass band and rousing sermons; and as far west as
Minnis Bay Anglican church.

The shortest journey was to the Birchington United
Reformed Church (URC), but it could accommodate very
few people and seemed to be full of old (and therefore
very uninteresting) people. Then there was the Methodist
church at Garlinge on the outskirts of Margate. Uncle
Mike and Auntie June lived in Garlinge when they were off
duty, so it was natural to occasionally attend that church
during my time at Barrington. The appointment of a young
Methodist minister initially promised a breath of fresh air
to the usual proceedings, but after just a few weeks it was
clear that nothing was really going to change. He seemed
enthusiastic and willing enough, but he was unable to
really connect with us. This wasn't helped by row after
vacant row of varnished pine pews stretching almost the

whole length of the sanctuary which separated him from us. The building had a distinctly empty feel that made me wonder at times why we were there if most of the Garlinge population failed to see the importance of attending.

Birchington Baptist was the church of my childhood years, that is between the ages of four and seventeen. This was interspersed with very occasional visits to the other churches mentioned above. The building itself accommodated about 120 people on a Sunday, and we children constituted up to half that number. The adults were mainly middle-aged or pensioners (reflecting the local demographics) with very few if any young adults or teenagers. In our view it was not difficult to see why. The order of service was solemn, formal and traditional, comprising the usual Baptist hymn-sermon sandwich supplemented each month by a communion service in which we did not participate.

Proceedings began with a change in organ music and hushed tones as the vestry door slowly swung open and the besuited deacons filed into the sanctuary, followed by the minister in his long flowing black robes, head reverently bowed, and gaze unblinkingly fixed on the floor about two feet ahead of him. The deacons then assumed their seating positions on the darkly varnished front pews while the minister carefully and solemnly climbed the pulpit steps, sat down, bowed his head in a short prayer, after which he surveyed the congregation in a 180-degree arc before standing to welcome us and announce the first hymn. It was very clear to us that the minister took his duties very seriously and expected us to behave appropriately.

To help us do so, our house-parents were expected to monitor our behaviour closely. We were expected to put away any items such as metal toys, dispense with chewing and bubble gum and stop swapping cards with each other featuring football players and other celebrities ('I've got Bobby Charlton; will you swap him for Martin Peters or Geoff Hurst?').

We managed to pay attention for the first 15 minutes or so, but then would start to fidget. Out came the cards as we surreptitiously passed them between ourselves. Discovery would mean immediate and irrevocable confiscation, so we were very careful to pass our cards under our legs and along the pew to complete the deals. And besides, this was far more exciting than singing old-fashioned and slow-moving hymns that we didn't fully understand. Occasionally, we would be invited to sing a chorus or song appropriate for our age such as 'Tell me the stories of Jesus I love to hear', but most of the time we uncomprehendingly half-sang and half-mumbled the hymns. We tried to relieve the boredom in various undetectable ways. For those with a penchant for arithmetic, the hymn numbers and lifespans of the composers offered fertile ground for working out averages and arithmetic distributions, etc. Others of us were more interested in people-watching, so our favourite pastime was to categorise the shapes and sizes of adult noses. This was very entertaining since members of the congregation seemed to display a wide variety of nose shapes. The object of the exercise was to identify how many nose types we could count and to guess if those adults with the same nose types were blood relatives. We knew that the minister had two sisters and all three had the same nose type. But there were others who were more difficult to place. In this way we injected some interest into the service. This became even more important when we reached 11 years of age because then we had to stay for the *whole* service – a mind-numbing one and a half hours of fidgeting, whispering, sniggering, crossing legs then uncrossing legs, and clearing out ear wax. In fact, anything that did not involve listening to the incomprehensible droning emanating from the gesticulating black robe in the pulpit. That was our perception at that age.

That being said, it is a curious fact that the minister was very well regarded in Baptist circles for his preaching and teaching ministry. He was a convert to Christianity from Judaism and specialised in relating the New Testament to the Old Testament. Unfortunately for him, but to our own great amusement, his surname and his unbelievably severe short-back-and-sides lent themselves nicely to the rather irreverent nickname 'Haircut'. His sermons were about 45–60 minutes in length and at times the hands of the clock seemed to be steadfastly stuck. By the time the last hymn had been sung and the blessing pronounced it was well past 12 o'clock. We would hurry out of the pews and along the aisle to wait impatiently on the pavement outside for our house-parents to emerge and then to commence the return walk to Barrington for the very welcome full Sunday roast that awaited us.

Regrettably, the roast dinner did not mark the end of our travails. We were also required to attend short services in the on-site chapel on both Sunday and Wednesday evenings. These services were far less traditional in every way. The chapel building was bright and airy, reflecting the 1960s era in which it was built. The pews were child-friendly as were the lightweight hymnals which included modern hymns and some choruses. The principal led the Wednesday service in a no-nonsense manner, but the Sunday services were often led by young trainee ministers from Spurgeon's College in south London. These trainees tended to conduct the services with a lighter and more interactive touch – they sometimes didn't even use the pulpit, instead choosing to stand below it on the dais at our level. Such services would typically comprise a short talk with a practical application and some review questions, plus three or four hymns.

Very occasionally some of the children were baptised 'on confession of their faith'. I wasn't sure what that really meant, but I do remember the baptism of Raymond who was the eldest son of one of the house-parents. He was in his teens at the time and was very large for his age. Two things stood out to me on that occasion. The first was that Raymond was very sincere about his faith, as was apparent from his explanation of how he had become a Christian and how that had changed his life; the second was the huge wave that he displaced, and which lapped over the baptistry edge on to the chapel floor as his substantial bulk disappeared under the water while the minister and assistant strained to heave him up again. I had seen nothing like it before! However, its spiritual impact on me was limited to an acknowledgement that some people became Christians, and it meant a lot to them.

The best Sundays were those when the principal announced at the end of the service that a kind benefactor had donated some money for sweets. These were then distributed as we left the chapel and were consumed in the playroom during the course of the evening as we listened to the last 15 minutes of the weekly Top 20 on BBC Radio 1.

On the whole, then, Sundays seemed to be full of things we didn't like but were forced to do – whether that was letter-writing to uncommunicative parents or the gnawingly boring interminable church services. Yes, the roast dinners and high teas were appreciated, but essentially Sundays, God and religion were boring and irrelevant.

Chapter 6

Who Cares?

According to available records there is no evidence that my mother ever took me home for the holidays. The correspondence between her and the Homes makes for depressing reading. In August 1963 when I was not yet 4 years old, the then principal Mr Addison wrote, *David is very disappointed . . . I hope you will make some effort to see him for a few days during the holidays. You will appreciate how much it means to our children to spend a holiday away.* The following summer the Homes wrote to my mother saying I was *the only child in his house who is not going away at all.* I had started primary school in September 1964 and seemed to *like it very much,* but I continued to wet the bed and my behaviour was still *difficult.*

On 26th November 1964 Mr Addison issued my mother with an ultimatum: *We are not satisfied with the interest and contact with David . . . unless you are prepared to show more interest in him we shall return him to you and will bring David on the train to Victoria station on Saturday 19th December to hand him over to you.* Receiving no reply, the Homes then wrote to my grandmother to ask her for information about my mother's whereabouts. In the meantime, I spent Christmas Day and Boxing Day with a 'friend' of the Homes, a Mrs B, to give me some kind of break. My grandmother could not explain my mother's silence, stating melodramatically in her letter, *something terrible must have happened!* The Homes urged my gran to visit me: *it is most important that he has some contact with his family.* She never visited but there was an initial burst of letters to me from her, her brother Gordon and sister Brenda during early 1965. But these soon tailed off. It seemed that my relatives weren't particularly interested in me.

My mother had disappeared, and my behaviour was causing concern. The Homes had issued an ultimatum that I would be returned to my mother. But had received no reply. Something had to change, and on Wednesday 2nd June 1965 it did.

At 8:30am that day my grandmother, Mrs Jean Spark, rang the Homes *very distraught and talking wildly.* My mother Virginia had appeared on her doorstep a few days earlier but refused to visit me or to speak to anyone on the phone. Mr and Mrs Addison arranged to visit that evening for an hour and a half, and their account of the visit vividly describes the serious state of my mother's health and the impact it had on them personally. It is therefore worth quoting in full.

> *We called to see Virginia at 7:30pm on 2nd June and were shown by Mrs Spark into a basement flat behind the shop at 136a High Street, Broadstairs. The room was crowded with an accumulation of junk and bric-a-brac, and Virginia, called by her mother, came in to*

see us. She had the appearance of both a child and old woman. She was unkempt, hair untidy, no make-up, pale and thin, eyes half closed and clouded, with drooping of one eye. Fingernails bitten right down. Dressed in trews, red boots, three cardigans, which were clean but old and shabby. Throughout our visit she sat slouched in a chair, rarely looked at us and constantly thumbed through an old and worn Reader's Digest.

This was not the Virginia we knew, who was a beautiful girl, always tidy and groomed, and composed beyond her years. We both knew immediately she was very sick in mind.

We put various questions to her concerning her health, whereabouts for the last ten months, and her lack of interest and responsibility towards David.

She told us she had no intention of visiting, writing or having any contact with him, that she just could not 'afford him'. When pointed out that financially she contributed nothing she said he had cost her health and means of work and to see him would only bring on all the tension and strain again. Asked what she would do if she was told she had to undertake responsibility for David she said she would put him in Barnardo's or a Council Home or send him on a plane to his father in Switzerland.

*She said she had no feeling for him whatever and she was not concerned that he had problems of his own or that she was the cause of his deprivation and unhappiness. She **would not** see him or take any interest.*

She was for the most part, rational, polite and well spoken. She has spent some time (nine weeks) in hospital at Horsham and talked of psychiatrists who had treated her with drugs, etc. She said she had stopped them as they made her feel giddy and queer and that she was not on them at present (we wonder!). She has a bedsitter at 11a Randolph Avenue, Maida Vale, W.9. But would not tell us whether she was working or how she paid to live. She does not know the name of her landlord but pays rent to another person.

She blames her trouble to:

1. *Lack of love from her mother as a child.*

2. *The War and its after effects (she was only a child at this time).*

3. *David's father for letting her down and the fact that she 'couldn't keep up with his people' when she went to Switzerland to marry him and returned after six months with the child and he was admitted to the Homes on 31.8.61.*

4. *The mother and baby home where she went in her pregnancy – 'Callous treatment', humiliated by remarks i.e., 'People who want children can't have them and those that shouldn't have them do, etc.'*

5. *'Appalling treatment at hospital – disgusting and crude agony of birth.'*

6. *'There should be a law against a man producing bastards and what was to be done about them*

– this country would be like Sweden' (each time she spoke irrationally about a law being needed against this and that and became very confused).

We told her to think again about David as she knew from bitter experience what it meant to be rejected by a mother. If she still does not wish to have anything to do with him she should contact his father to see if he would be prepared to offer him a home.

We came to the conclusion that Virginia is ill and it would be wrong to force her to see David who is himself emotionally disturbed and only further harm could result. We told her we would like to help her but came away disheartened and grieved to know that the girl was in such a state of instability and despondency.

There had over the years been hints in correspondence with the Homes that my mother's health was fragile. But this visit persuaded all concerned that she was now seriously ill and would be unable to relate to me in ways that would normally be expected of a mother. I was at this time only five and a half years old.

The Homes encouraged my gran to visit me and stated that it could make visiting hours *very flexible.* But her responses were disappointing: *My work keeps me busy . . . like many of my relations he will have to see me when I am free.* This from a close relative who lived no more than seven miles from the Homes. The 'work' she refers to is clairvoyance and I was later to learn that this work meant everything to her.

I remember staying at my gran's place overnight as a young child, the one and only time this happened. I was so frightened by the experience that I hardly slept a wink and was repelled by the stench and filth produced by the various animals she kept. My grandmother was therefore not a suitable person to be involved in my upbringing. The Homes probably felt compelled to approach her as my next of kin, but I know for certain that Miss Mary was relieved that my gran took no real interest in me, and I was therefore spared further contact. I am certain Mr and Mrs Addison felt the same way, having experienced at first hand both my grandmother's often bizarre behaviour and the squalor in which she lived.

So within a week of meeting my mother, the Homes approached my father in Basel, Switzerland. Up until this point his direct contact with me was confined to sending presents at Christmas. My mother kept him regularly informed of how I was doing but he never corresponded directly with me. However, he did begin writing to the Homes in December 1964 in order to establish my mother's whereabouts, as he too had lost contact with her. He also asked Miss Mary to tell him *a little about David* and *how he is doing* and hopes that the Christmas parcel *will please him, and maybe he will remember where it comes from.*

Things changed, however, after the Addisons met my mother on 2nd June. Mr Addison wrote to my father on 6th June explaining the new situation and asking him to make plans to care for me. He replied on 6th July saying that he could not look after me because of his financial situation and the need to work (recurring themes in his letters). He also states that it was my mother who *insisted to care for* me and leaves it to Mr Addison to work things out. The correspondence continues into November 1965 with my father insisting that Mr Addison resolve the situation and repeating that he could not for financial and legal reasons care for me primarily because my mother had legal custody. Mr Addison encourages him to visit me in person, but he declines, saying that he needs my mother's express permission to do so and, in any case, is unable to do so. He then states that my mother is in breach of her contract with him to look after me and threatens to take the matter to the British Consul to force the Homes to resolve the issue of my care due to my mother's illness.

At this time my mother was still in hospital receiving treatment while also looking for a job, but unable to have me visit for the holidays. It was now 12 months since she had last seen me and since the Homes had issued its ultimatum.

This was all quite rightly concealed from me as a five-year-old. But this lack of family care for me almost certainly contributed to concerns about my behaviour. As Mr Addison wrote to my father in November 1965: *Although David is well, he has been emotionally disturbed due to the lack of parental interest in him.* Two aspects of my behaviour are regularly noted from age three to six. First, I liked *undivided attention,* and if I did not get it then I got *put out and upset very quickly* and my behaviour *deteriorated* into *temper tantrums.* Clearly, I craved attention, perfectly understandable since I was getting precious little from my relatives! Second, I was wetting the bed *although every attempt has been made to help* me. This meant that I could not stay overnight at Mrs B's home. Mrs B also described me as *not an easy child*, a significant negative evaluation of my behaviour as a five-year-old since she had taken it upon herself to visit me on visiting days and have me visit her during the holidays. So she was well disposed towards me, yet even she was finding my behaviour difficult to manage. During the summer of 1965 my behaviour and attitude to life had *deteriorated,* and during Christmas 1965 I spent the holiday in sickbay *under observation for incontinence.* The following February I underwent tests at Margate hospital for my bedwetting: the Homes were clearly concerned and for good reason – if not for my incontinence, they would be able to introduce me to more 'Friends'. The Easter report about me says that I was making slightly more effort but that I had had only two dry nights that term. The hospital results were negative: there was nothing wrong with me physically. The reason for my incontinence was either emotional or volitional. Either way, I was clearly a deeply troubled child.

Despite this I was introduced to some other 'Friends' of the Homes. These were, like Mrs B, people who took an interest in a child's welfare by visiting, providing holidays, writing letters and giving presents. During early 1966 Mrs B continued to visit me regularly. The sum total of interest from my relatives was a solitary Easter card from my gran, and I again stayed at the Homes during the Easter holidays. I was then introduced to Mr and Mrs W from Wimborne, Dorset. They sent me a jacket which I was *thrilled to have* and was *so pleased to have something of [my] own which is different from anything other children have.* I remember the jacket well – it was a fur-lined suede 'car coat' – and it definitely lifted my mood.

Mrs B continued to welcome me every visiting day, and the Dorset couple continued to send me presents. But there was no contact from my parents, and in a letter to my father in March 1966 Mrs Addison stated her deep concerns about me: *We have been extremely worried about David's position for a long time as he has been abandoned by his own people.* I was introduced to two further Friends during the summer: Miss M of Gillingham and Miss D of Ilford. They both visited me during the summer holiday, but the summer report stated: *David still wet every night; behaviour spasmodic.* The attention I received was welcome enough, but it was clearly going to take far more than visits and presents from well-wishers to help me.

Mrs B and the Dorset couple continued their interest in me at Christmas time that year: *[David] has been absolutely thrilled [with the gifts] and has been the envy of some of the other children.* By contrast, my gran sent three parcels and letters although I received *nothing from other relatives.* The Christmas report states that I was keeping very fit and that my school progress was excellent. But it noted that my behaviour was still a concern and finished on a telling note: *No more contact with father.* The Homes were not to hear from him ever again.

Chapter 7

'A Very Disturbed Little Boy'

In February 1967, now aged seven, I was transferred from The Dingle to a new house in Block 3 called Barrington. This was standard practice at the Homes, the idea being that I should grow up under the care of a man as well as a woman. This was particularly necessary in my case because I could be rough with the younger children in The Dingle. The new house-parents were a couple in their late 20s known to us as Uncle Mike and Auntie June. They had two children of their own and were assisted by Miss Heather Brown who acted as their relief when they were off duty. I stayed in Barrington for about ten years, so these three adults were to be very formative influences on me during my time at the Homes.

By this time, I had stopped wetting myself during the daytime but was still struggling at night. Mike and June termed it *David's nasty habit* in their official notes. Something had to be done: incontinence not only corroded my own self-esteem but also limited my prospects of being fostered or adopted. Furthermore, it could be seen as an affront to the Homes' efforts to instil in me discipline and self-control. For these reasons a multipronged attack was launched on this scourge.

Soon after moving to Barrington, my behaviour at school became so disruptive that I was taken to see a certain Dr F. I'd been ejected from music lessons because I insisted on treating my wooden recorder like a football whistle and because I had hit another child. I did not trust Dr F, initially because his long white coat and the mirror he wore on his head made him look distinctly odd, but later because a (false) confidence I shared with him made its way back to Mike and June.

A variety of techniques were tried with little effect and I made a huge effort too because of the humiliation I felt. All my peers were dry, and the older I got, the more they teased me, which resulted in greater embarrassment. For whatever reason, I just didn't seem to be able to stop wetting the bed most nights.

Another habit I could not break was my fascination with fire. No matter how many times I was reminded of its dangers, I found it almost mesmerising. I was also a thief, and one night these three elements came together in a very dangerous way. I'd woken up during the night feeling wet, cold and hungry, so I quietly and carefully made my way down to the main kitchen. It was a risky venture because at any point I could be detected and would face a severe punishment. However, it was the dead of night, so I relaxed as I realised that no one was likely to be awake. On reaching the kitchen I found there was little to eat by way of leftovers from the day's meals. I opened the huge double-doors of the fridge and my eyes focused past the huge aluminium jugs of milk and fixed on my favourite food – sausages! I lit the gas stove and found a frying pan. But after several minutes the sausages didn't seem to be sizzling as I knew they should. They remained stubbornly cold with burnt edges: I was clearly doing something wrong, so I reluctantly gave up on my idea of a midnight feast. But I took a large box of kitchen matches to play with, and once under my bed clothes began to strike them one at a time as if under canvas. By the time I'd finished the box I had unwittingly burnt a sizeable hole in the top sheet. I panicked and decided to get rid of the evidence by flushing the burnt matches down the toilet. To my horror they kept floating back to the surface despite repeated flushes of water. I then tried scooping them up and stuffing them down the wash basin plug holes, only to find they snapped under the pressure and could not be pushed down out of sight. In the end I did my best to cover my tracks, returned to bed and fell asleep.

The following morning revealed a very obvious trail of burnt matches leading from my bedside to the bathroom. I therefore had to admit to my misdemeanour, knowing that I faced a very severe punishment. Breakfast and lunch passed uneventfully but on arriving home for tea I was summoned to the principal's office. I was so naive that I didn't know what to expect. Even so, for some reason I was trembling when I knocked on the office door and entered. Mr Addison was sitting before me wearing a very stern expression. He checked the facts. Had I been in the kitchen cooking sausages that night? Yes, I had. Had I turned on the gas? Yes, I had. Feeling increasingly nervous I lifted my fingers to bite my nails only to drop them sharply as Mr Addison's small cane descended painfully on my knuckles. He was clearly very angry, and I was a very frightened eight-year-old. It seems that in my haste to get back to bed I had forgotten to turn off some of the unlit gas taps.

The first cook to arrive that morning – a Mrs C – had not detected the smell. She was just about to light the gas when Mr Mac, a house-parent who rose early, entered and, smelling the gas, prevented what could have been a catastrophic explosion. No wonder Mr Addison was so angry! I can't remember much more about the meeting except that I was told in no uncertain terms that I would be sent to a Borstal (a prison-like children's centre) if anything remotely like this happened again. I left Mr Addison's presence completely shaken, but I had learnt a very, very important lesson!

The most obvious reason for my incontinence was because I was emotionally disturbed, and, as I have mentioned, these psychological difficulties reduced my chances of being fostered or adopted. The Homes were making considerable efforts in this direction, and during the years 1967–68 Mr and Mrs W continued their interest in me. I stayed with them during the summer of 1967 because I was, in Mr Addison's words, receiving *no parental interest*. Indeed, during 1967 my mother visited only once, and although she offered to have me for five days over Christmas that year, she allowed Mr and Mrs W to take me for the whole holiday of 19 days, accepting that she was *out of touch* with me. I was quietly relieved and enjoyed staying with Mr and Mrs W.

The Christmas went well and they invited me for the following Easter holiday and were due to pick me up in London after the annual pageant on 5th April 1968. This was a spectacular dramatic production featuring us children. Mr Addison had sent Mr and Mrs W two tickets for the event stating *I hope you will enjoy what you see and hear.* Unfortunately, what they saw and heard that evening from me was far from enjoyable! All I remember is that when they came to collect me that night, I had a sudden panic attack. For some unknown reason I felt completely insecure and wanted to return to the Homes. I remember crying my eyes out and firmly planting myself cross-legged in the road adjacent to the main concourse of Victoria railway station. I refused to be persuaded, cajoled or physically removed until I was assured that I would not be forced to go with Mr and Mrs W. The exasperated Homes staff very reluctantly agreed to take me back with them.

At the time, all I could think of were my own feelings, but in retrospect Mr and Mrs W must have been very disappointed and confused, and the Homes' staff deeply embarrassed. According to the written apology sent by Mr Addison three days later, it seemed that I had not wanted to compete for Mr and Mrs W's attention with two other children who were also invited. That may just have been my way of offering an excuse that I thought would be acceptable. Whatever the reason, Mr Addison offered his *sincere regrets* and recommended that Mr and Mrs W discontinue the visits and holidays but keep corresponding with me.

Uncle Mike and Auntie June were also experiencing difficulties with me at this time. Their April 1968 report states that *David is the biggest problem in the house. He is very dishonest, playing silly jokes . . . He's a thief and a bully with the younger children.* The only positive point made was, according to my teacher, that *[David is] brighter than his years.* But Mike and June conclude that I was nonetheless *a very disturbed little boy.* It was around this time that the sausages and gas incident occurred. My bedwetting was also *still very unpleasant,* and although by December I was under Dr F the psychiatrist, Mike and June noted that there *has not been any improvement.* I spent Christmas with a young clergyman and his wife in the north London suburb of New Barnet, but never once felt any desire to trade the Homes for their small two-bedroom flat and, it seemed to me, their humdrum lifestyle. Apparently, I *created a lot of fuss returning* – another abortive if well-intentioned attempt to get me linked to potential foster carers and adopters. By this time I had also severed my links with Mrs B on the grounds that I had grown to dislike her husband. All in all, five families had shown an interest in me, and I took to none of them. Given all this and especially Mike and June's observation that *I was a very disturbed little boy,* it was unsurprising that during the summer of 1969 I was admitted to Lanthorne House children's psychiatric hospital. I was then nine years old.

The great thing about Lanthorne was that there was little pressure to do anything that I didn't want to. There must have been dozens of other children there, so I happily fitted in with the daily routines of waking, washing, eating and going to classes. I don't recall doing any chores – which was a welcome change – but I do remember having to take my place in the queue each morning for my large spoonful of sweet green Minadex vitamin medicine. I really enjoyed myself at Lanthorne; the weather was sunny and the sprawling grounds meant we could play to our hearts' content. In fact, the staff were very friendly and chatty. What I didn't realise at the time was that they were observing and evaluating my mental state. After three months I was discharged and returned to the Homes to face another long summer holiday.

But this time my mother was well enough to take me on a week's caravan holiday near Sandwich, Kent. It was the first time in three years that my mother's mental health was remotely stable. My great uncle Gordon came along too, and he taught me many card tricks and games while we were forced inside by the rain. It was the first time I had met him, and I enjoyed listening to his jokes and playing with the large shiny ball bearings he gave me which he'd acquired as a breaker of London Transport buses. For the first time I began to understand who my other relatives were. Gordon was my gran's younger brother, and also brother of Brenda, the second-eldest sibling, who also lived in London.

We went for walks along the beach and the golf course and enjoyed the occasional ice cream and meal out. However, this turned out to be the one and only holiday I ever spent with my mother or any of my relatives. I enjoyed the holiday and would have liked to have met my other relatives too at some point. But as time went on I assumed that they were not interested in getting to know me and had their own busy lives to get on with.

My stay at Lanthorne was very positive: Mike and June recorded that my treatment at Lanthorne had done me *the world of good,* and that I was *fairly reliably dry* and *genuinely happy all round.* The Homes therefore introduced me to a couple from Gillingham who took a keen interest in me. My mother visited every month or two and wrote an occasional letter during 1970–71. Sadly, the contact with the Gillingham couple ceased abruptly without my knowing why, although Auntie June later confided that, in her opinion, they were unsuitable, and she was glad for my sake. I continued to improve, becoming a *very much more stable, happy normal boy.*

Chapter 8

'King Eths'

My schoolwork was also improving. In fact, I was considered *very intelligent,* although my 11+ exam results were only good enough to get me into the top sets at the local secondary school, King Ethelbert's, rather than into a grammar school. I was not alone in this: I am aware of only two or three other children from the Homes who passed the 11+ around this time. I wasn't unhappy with the situation: I already knew lots of the children at King Eths (as we called the school). This meant I had a ready-made peer group and could rely on some of the older children for protection against any bullies. This sense of solidarity was really important to all of us at King Eths because we closed ranks and protected each other against any of our peers who mocked us for being at the Homes. After all, exactly what kind of parent would put us in a children's home unless there was something badly wrong with us! We felt they had a point. But we also knew that we could not concede that or allow any of us to be singled out for bullying. So we closed ranks and our sheer numbers deterred most from trying their luck.

The first year at King Eths was uneventful as I got used to the routine demands and expectations of being at 'big school'. It was a large co-educational school, catering for 800 pupils, and had been built in 1938 for a very broad range of educational abilities. This was recognised by the introduction of the Certificate of Secondary Education (CSE) with grades of 1–5. This was awarded by means of continuous assessment and formal time-limited exams. Its purpose was to ensure that every child left school with a certificate of some kind. With grade 3 being average, grade 1 was considered to be the equivalent of a General Certificate of Education (GCE) O (i.e. Ordinary) level certificate, usually awarded to abler pupils attending grammar, private and technical schools.

The students in the bottom sets for English and Maths were destined (some would say, doomed) to leave school with few formal qualifications and limited job prospects. Those of us who managed grade 3 or above would fare better but would still be unable to go on to take the Ordinary or Advanced (A) level certificates that promised much greater opportunities in adult life. There were two reasons for this. First, there was only one subject taught to O-level standard, and the teacher was more often absent than present. Second, we were not expected to aspire to O- and A-level standards of education. It was understood that the grammar system creamed off the most able for university entry, and that secondary modern pupils were expected to settle for the humble CSE.

But it wasn't just the school's modest expectations that shaped so many of our young lives. Most of my fellow pupils had low expectations of themselves, whether as a result of their parents' low expectations or of their relatively disadvantaged social and economic circumstances. This was hardly surprising given that many of the children came from large council housing estates in Birchington.

So, for many children school was a chore to be tolerated. Their main objective was to do the required work without too much fuss and leave school as soon as possible in order to earn some money and have a good time like those who had attended King Eths before them. For a small minority, school was to be actively resisted – sometimes violently. The school set out the expected standards of behaviour, with sanctions for misbehaviour. Most incidents were dealt with informally by class teachers by way of extra work, detention or removal of break-time or other privileges. Persistent offenders had their names entered into the school 'Conduct Book'.

This was to be avoided given that the Conduct Book was held by the deputy head, the fearsome Mr Tuppen, who made his presence felt from day one at school. He it was who patrolled the school stage when we filed into the school assembly hall each morning. He stood right at the edge of the stage, occasionally rising on to his toes and jutting out his chin as his icy stare caused a whispering or fidgeting student to immediately desist. After all, his reputation preceded him, and no one ever wanted to experience the excruciating swish of his cane.

Whenever we were sent to Mr Tuppen to collect the Conduct Book, we were required to explain what we had done to deserve it. He was an unsmiling, austere fifty-something ex-army major with absolutely no time for misdemeanours and misconduct. He was responsible for administering two, four or six strokes of his short, flexible and exceedingly painful cane, should any of us be unwise enough to be named in the Conduct Book three times in any one term. Mr Tuppen did not hold back. He quite literally put his back into his caning duties and the prospect of having to explain ourselves was a real incentive to behave or, at the very least, avoid being caught. The problem was that there were just too many irresistible opportunities to play pranks on each other, and as we progressed from the first to the third year (Year 9), my friends and I began to assert our authority over the younger students and behave in ways that could result in a visit to Mr Tuppen.

Sadly, my good start at school did not last: my report from the Homes for Christmas 1972 read, *terrible term for David. He is argumentative, has the last word in everything and will not take any criticism. He is developing signs of [sic] persecution . . . Does not work to his ability. He has been caught stealing from the village shop. Dr Martin (the local GP) considers him to be very immature.* I was, in short, going through a period of teenage rebellion.

Chapter 9

More Answers, More Questions

Since going on holiday with me and Uncle Gordon my mother wrote and occasionally sent money, but she didn't visit, and never had me to stay. I didn't know it at the time but she had become seriously ill again and had been 'sectioned' to secure accommodation for her own protection. So when I was about 13 years old, a couple from Edgware, London, began taking an interest in me. Mike and June commenting in mid-1973 stated that *David has improved . . . This ties in with the interest shown in him by Mr and Mrs S. This is really what David needs, someone who takes an interest in him alone.*

They were right. Mr and Mrs S were wealthy and generous, and I enjoyed being pampered. But, unknown to me, they were dissatisfied with this arrangement. In correspondence dated June 1973, Mrs S informed Mr Honey (the new principal) that *frankly we did not expect the child to be so old . . . We would have wished for a much younger child on a more permanent basis. It is easier to give love to children when you can cuddle them!* Mr Honey responded by saying: *We fully understand how you feel concerning the difficulties of having an older child . . . If you feel that David is too old, please have no hesitation in making this clear when you visit us . . .*

It probably hadn't helped that I had also made it clear to them that I could only acknowledge my birth mother as my true mother and so, after six months and without warning, they suddenly ceased contact. I was now 13 years old and therefore unlikely to ever be adopted. It was then that I realised that I still felt a strong if deeply ambivalent emotional attachment to my mother. And it was about six months after Mr and Mrs S dropped me that my father was mentioned – but *not* by one of the staff.

We often gathered around the TV to watch a programme called *Ski Sunday*. On one occasion we were watching a Swiss skier take his starting position when one of the boys, Colin, said to me, 'That's your dad!' To which I replied, 'What do you mean?' 'Well, he's Swiss, isn't he?' I said, 'I don't know. How do *you* know?' 'Well, I heard Auntie and Uncle talking about him.'

I was dumbfounded. I really didn't know what to think. I made a mental note of this, but it took another 18 months when I was then aged 15 to realise that I *needed* some answers. I needed to make sense of whose child I was and who I was. This need had been gnawing away at me since I had turned 13, but the house-parents had no information to give me except to confirm that my father was indeed Swiss. So, I tried to fill in the blanks in two different ways. First, I constructed an idealised picture of my father: he had been a famous journalist whose job took him to faraway places, and this had caused the breakdown in my parent's relationship. So, he was a flawed hero, but a hero all the same. Second, I used to gaze intently into the mirror and try to identify those parts of my face that I had inherited from my mother and then extrapolate my father's features from what remained. It wasn't a very successful exercise, and I was left none the wiser. But it was nice to know I had a dad and that he was Swiss (and therefore probably rich!), and the idealised story helped me to cope with my unanswered questions.

What I didn't realise at the time (and didn't discover until I was in my mid-40s) was that during the summer of 1975 my mother had prompted John Honey to write to a Dr Kurt Yenny in Basel, Switzerland. Dr Kurt worked for a Swiss fiduciary company responsible for administering money that my father had agreed to pay and that would be mine on my 18th birthday. It was probably this issue that Colin had heard discussed in some form. Whatever the case, John Honey decided that it was time for my mother to provide some answers, and she duly agreed to meet me at St Augustine's psychiatric hospital near Canterbury, Kent, at 6pm on Tuesday 3rd June 1975.

I remember that day very well. This was my opportunity to put my questions to her.

It was a beautiful summer evening as John Honey drove me into the grounds of the whitewashed Victorian building known as St Augustine's Hospital. He had arranged with the hospital authorities to leave me in the rear passenger seat of his white four-seater Renault 16 and for my mother to join me there. So, I waited patiently. I hadn't seen her for four years and I was shocked to see that she had aged considerably. She looked like a woman approaching her 50s rather than the 35-year-old that she was. She wore a nondescript pale-blue dress and, with seemingly uncomprehending eyes, looked directly forward and slightly down. Her arms hung stiffly down her sides and she shuffled at a slow, even pace towards me. I was instinctively repulsed and braced myself to cope with this strange and clearly unwell woman who was my mother. To be frank, I would have wished it otherwise: for her to be well, or to be unwell and not my mother. But I had to face reality and I needed answers, so I did my best to control my feelings and to be sensitive to hers. This was probably a day she had been dreading for some time. It would have been challenging enough for a mother in good mental health to explain to her 15-year-old son why he had been in care for more than 13 years. She must have wondered what my reaction to her would be. Would I be angry, violent, silent, dismissive? Would I ridicule her, blame her, even disown her?

It may be, however, that she felt she owed me an explanation, whatever the possible repercussions. I think this is how Mr Honey would have put it to her, especially since it was by no means certain that I would ever meet my father to hear his version of events. So she slowly eased herself in and sat next to me and falteringly recounted her sorry story as she fidgeted and looked anywhere but at me. My mother's explanation was fragmented and at times incoherent. I couldn't then understand the devastating impact on her of ten years of paranoid schizophrenia and the bludgeoning effect of the powerful drugs that were necessary to prevent her from completely losing her mind. But I concentrated hard and listened to what she had to say.

She had met my father, Walter, in London in the late 50s. He was from Switzerland and was improving his English while working for a well-known tea merchant. It seems that they had met on more than one occasion but by mid-1959 my mother knew she was pregnant. They were both 20 years old and unmarried. During the pregnancy, my father returned to Switzerland. In early 1961, my mother took me to Switzerland where she tried to persuade my father to marry her. She persisted in this for six months until August that year when she returned despondently to the UK. My father's parents felt that he should marry my mother, but he steadfastly refused and eventually agreed to take out an insurance policy that would provide for me financially when I reached maturity.

It was on our return to the UK that my mother wrote to the Homes, asking the principal to take me in due to her ill-health and inability to both earn a living and care for me.

Those were the days when unmarried mothers were stigmatised (as were their illegitimate children), and state support was insufficient to permit single mothers to care for their children and work at the same time. The preferred option at that time was to have a child like me put up for adoption. But the hoped-for reconciliation with my father had never happened and my mother's health remained poor, so I had remained in care. She also explained that she had only rarely visited me at the Homes because initially it was expensive and time-consuming to travel the 72 miles from London every fortnight and because her mental health had completely broken down when I was about five years old. For six years after this she had received outpatient care at various National Health Service facilities until 1970 when her psychiatrist sectioned her under the Mental Health Act for her own protection. This was the reason why she had not visited me at all for the previous four years.

As a 15-year-old I did not really understand mental illness. How could I? But on that day, I could see that she was heavily medicated. Physically she moved very slowly, and her speech was slow, halting and monotone. It took a real effort on my part to be patient and wait for her to collect her thoughts and compose answers to my questions. No, she didn't know where my father lived now, and she had not heard from him for years. But his last known address was in the northern Swiss town of Riehen. So at age 15 I had answers to at least some of my questions.

I now knew why I was in the Homes, and that my absent father was indeed Swiss and was alive. The meeting helped me understand my past, but it didn't help me plan my future. This is probably why my mother agreed to the meeting and asked John Honey to enquire about the financial provision made for me. The years were ticking by inexorably, and I would be taking my final school exams in the following summer of 1976. At that point, I could legally leave school and the Homes. But I would be on my own, and the future beyond that date was a very worrying mental blank.

My mother wasn't the only one who was concerned for my future, and this became apparent at school when my friends and I were summoned yet again to Mr Tuppen's office for a dressing down. But this time, things were different. After dismissing my friends, Mr Tuppen unexpectedly instructed me to stay behind. I quivered and expected the worst. What hidden misdemeanour had now come to light? Instead, his expression changed from one of disinterested detachment to one of real pastoral concern. I can remember his words very clearly: 'Meader, you are an intelligent lad. But you have a choice. You can continue to play up with your friends and leave the school having failed to reach your potential, or you can choose to apply yourself and leave with good grades and good prospects. The choice is yours.'

At the time, I was just relieved to get away from him pain-free. But later it struck me that he was genuinely concerned that I would squander my talents for the sake of being popular and daring. His words made a deep impact on me. Here was a headteacher with a reputation for being aloof and merciless showing genuine concern for my welfare. I was puzzled. But this incongruence caused me for the first time to reflect deeply: what did I need to achieve at school before I left the Homes, at which point my school qualifications would form the main hope for something beyond a low-paid low-skilled job? It was a turning point for me, and I began to seriously think about life after school and after the Homes.

Over the years I had toyed with the idea of becoming a policeman, engine driver, police forensics officer and a sea captain. I remember a 15-minute careers advice interview given in the fourth year by a certain Mrs T who asked me, 'What do you want to be when you leave school?' I thought about this for a moment and brightly replied, 'An astrophysicist.' I was genuine enough (if rather naïve), having recently read widely on astronomy and particle physics and had become enthralled by the subject. For some reason she seemed rather taken aback but recovered herself, saying rather sardonically, 'And how many O-levels are you taking?' 'Only one,' I replied, completely missing the point of her question. Undeterred by my naivete, she pressed on: 'Have you thought of the Armed Forces?' She clearly didn't take my aspirations seriously, which isn't entirely surprising. After all, I was a child in care at a secondary school and expected to achieve only CSE grades. To be fair to her, though, she was justified in making her suggestion because by this time I had joined the Margate Sea Cadets as an introduction to a possible Royal Navy career.

Each week I pressed my uniform creases using an iron over brown paper, and then cycled the six-mile round trip to the Cadet HQ on my newly acquired second-hand bicycle. This lasted for about two years, culminating in a series of interviews with the Royal Navy with a view to becoming an Artificer's apprentice. Like many Spurgeon's teenagers before me, my thinking was that the Navy would give me a roof over my head and a trade which I could use in civilian life. I therefore opted for an electrician's apprenticeship which would enable me to do electrical work on leaving the Navy. But it was not to be. I was found to be colour blind and declined the alternative offer of a marine engineering apprenticeship. My Navy career was dead in the water.

I had taken Mr Tuppen's advice about achieving my educational potential and had therefore kept my options open should the Navy option lead nowhere. In those days, it was common for virtually all King Eths students to leave school as soon as they could, at age 16. For many, the appeal was two-fold: freedom from adult supervision, and the prospect of disposable income to buy nice things to impress the girls and have a good time. But to me, the only prospect I could see was low-paid and unfulfilling work. True, there was a certain superficial attraction to leaving school but unlike my peers I didn't have parental support or a family home to fall back on. I also realised that I could only measure my true potential by facing stiffer academic challenges than those offered by King Eths. It was clear I needed to move to a school that offered a full range of certificates. So, in early 1976 I discussed my plans with Mr Teasdale, the King Eths headteacher, and he agreed to support my application to a local technical high school if I achieved at least three grade 1 CSEs.

Mr Teasdale was as good as his word. On 13th August 1976, he wrote to the headteacher of Dane Court School in Broadstairs, asking him to consider my request *favourably* which he was sure *would be appreciated by all concerned*. I was interviewed at 3:30pm on Wednesday 1st September and started my O-level studies a few days later. I had cleared my first major hurdle.

Looking back, the two pivotal events that helped me most during my early teens were the meeting with my mother and the concerned words of advice from Mr Tuppen. Both of these occurred when I was 15 years old. I became more focused on my school studies and my behaviour improved significantly. By Christmas 1975 Mike and June reported that my bedwetting had *virtually disappeared*, that I had stopped bullying younger children, and that I was *very helpful* and *maturing very well*.

This progress came even though I was continuing to spend every holiday at the Homes and seeing virtually nothing of my mother. In fact, Mike and June commented that *there is very little between them and David appears embarrassed by her presence.* They were right. I *was* embarrassed by my mother and our relationship was a pale shadow of what it might have been under more favourable circumstances.

When she visited during the years 1975–77, she would always arrive after Saturday lunch and adopt the same routine that included a visit to a local cafe. The conversation was always stilted and awkward, and because we had so little in common it was punctuated by long silences. She seldom looked me in the eye, preferring instead to fix her gaze on a distant point beyond the café window or ahead of her when we were walking. She drew heavily and frequently on her cigarettes, narrowing her eyes and nervously flicking the ash into the ashtray. From time to time she would sip her coffee or tea, sometimes raising a teaspoon to her lips, and at other times fingering the crockery nervously, at a loss to know what to do or say next. Whether we walked along the local coastal paths or sat in a café eating cake or (in my case) a huge ice cream, the interaction was awkward and uncertain, our conversation merely a ritual both of us felt obliged to perform:

Mum: *How are you, David?*

Me: I'm well.

Mum: *How are you doing at school?*

Me: I'm doing well.

Mum: *What are your favourite subjects?*

Me: English, Geography and History.

Mum:	*What are you going to do when you leave school?*
Me:	I don't know. Maybe take some more exams.
Mum:	*You really should leave school and get a job. Like me and your grandmother did.*
Me:	(Pause: thinking, 'You don't understand!') But I can get a better job if I stay at school.
Mum:	*I really think it's time you got a job, David.*
Me:	If I leave now, I will get a low-paid dead-end job with nowhere to live and be stuck in this area.
Mum:	*You could come to London.*
Me:	(Pause: thinking, 'I don't know London or anyone in it. I'm only 16 years old for goodness' sake!') I don't like London and I want to get a good job.
Mum:	(Taking one last drag and stubbing out the cigarette butt in the glass ashtray.) *Come on, I think it's time we went back!*
Me:	(Thinks: 'I can't wait to get back!')

This is typical of our interactions: it was almost inevitable that we could not understand each other's point of view. After all, in the 16 years of my life I had spent only one week with my mother that I could draw on as a shared experience. We had lived parallel lives, and although we were genetically related and physically resembled each other there was little else that connected us. Worse than that, I was indeed embarrassed by her. Yes, I knew that she was still mentally ill, but that was no consolation to me when people shot sympathetic looks at me and each other as we walked around Birchington and Margate.

My grandmother was no better. She immersed herself in her own little world of horoscopes, crystal balls and occult practices, and berated me for not leaving school to earn a living. It seemed that both my mother and her mother were completely incapable of taking my aspirations seriously.

Chapter 10

Leaving, But Not Leaving

Nonetheless, I was making good academic progress. Dane Court took educational attainment seriously and, to be fair to King Eths, had the resources and staff to support that ethos. We were expected to apply ourselves and take responsibility for our learning. Dane Court students were better behaved and motivated than their King Eths counterparts, and the teachers were therefore able to focus more on teaching than on managing disruptive behaviour. I was highly motivated despite the disapproval of my mother and grandmother, because I felt that in order to reach my potential I had ultimately to obtain a university degree. At that time, only 1 in 7 school leavers went to university, so it would not be easy. But I would take each step at a time and see what I was capable of. The O-levels were challenging and required a lot of work, but I enjoyed my new learning environment. I was motivated by a combination of aspiration to greater things and the real fear of failure. I frequently pondered what I was going to do and how well I was likely to fare once the Spurgeon's gates finally closed behind me in 1977. I knew that the answer to those questions largely depended on me. Once I left the Homes I would be on my own. It was a hugely daunting prospect, and I didn't know if or how I would cope.

What I also didn't know at the time was that the future for the Homes was as uncertain as mine. Government policy was moving towards a very different model of social care based on small family-sized units of no more than a few children and away from the large-scale institutional care typified by the Homes. So the mid-to-late 1970s witnessed a rapid but managed decline in the number of social services referrals to the Homes, and one by one individual houses were closed down due to the drop in numbers. The houses in Block 1 were the first to close and the staff made redundant. At the same time, the Trustees were making plans to sell the Birchington site in order to fund the purchase of smaller properties throughout the UK. We would all be leaving Birchington sooner or later, whether we liked it or not.

Thankfully, John Honey had also been giving some thought to my transition into the wider world. The usual route was for those reaching school leaving age to be placed back home with a parent or parents, or to move straight into some kind of employment. In both cases the children ceased to be the Homes' responsibility, although there was no guarantee as to how they would subsequently fare. In some cases, the family would be dysfunctional, needy or violent, often with a single parent struggling to make ends meet. Others would enter the Armed Forces, moving from one form of institutional care to another, appreciating the familiarity of rules, discipline and routine, and the security of camaraderie, board, lodging and money. Most were happy to leave the Homes as soon as they could, and looked forward to the formal farewell service in the chapel when they would be presented with two sets of clothes, a suitcase, a small King James Bible and a prized £20 note.

From time to time 'Old Scholars', as they were known, would visit the Homes to say a heartfelt 'thank you' for the care they had received, often stating that at the time they had not appreciated just how good the care had been. But most were never seen or heard of once they passed through the gates for the final time. So I had no idea of what life was like for them and how well I was likely to do. What *was* clear to me was that I was at a distinct disadvantage. I had no parents, relatives or siblings to support me, no family home to live in and no employment. The one attempt to link me up with one of my mother's cousins in Farnham, Surrey, came to nothing. And so when I reached my 17th birthday, it was decided, with my consent, that I should be fostered by a couple who lived locally and who I shall call Mr and Mrs Masters.

This meant that I would be living in familiar surroundings and could continue my O-levels at the same school. The initial agreement was for 18 months starting January 1977, with the Homes underwriting the cost of food, lodging, clothes and pocket money. My character at the time was described as *maturing well* and *reliable*, so everything was set to make the placement successful.

I had my own small bedroom at the front of the three-bedroom house and tended to migrate there to study and listen to the radio or to play my vinyl LPs. Mr and Mrs Masters were a kindly couple and ensured that I got up in time for breakfast and the school bus and that my tea was waiting for me when I arrived home each evening. They were very keen that I should study as much as possible, being acutely aware that if I failed my O-levels I would not be able to progress to A-levels and university. I was also aware of this. But I was, after all, a teenager and I also felt the tug of two competing pursuits.

One of these was my love of chess which had developed during the long summer holidays. Uncle Mike had taught me to play at the age of ten and I subsequently put together six complete sets from the bits and pieces donated to the Homes. These six sets and the space provided by the quarter-size snooker table enabled me to play the opening variations simultaneously side-by-side. With the help of books borrowed from the local library I was able to entertain myself for hours during the lonely holidays at no cost. I eventually joined the local chess club that met in the Powell Arms pub in the main square. And I loved the drama played out internationally between Bobby Fischer and Boris Spassky. Bobby Fischer was well-known for his unpredictable behaviour off the board and his brilliance on the board. His showdown with Boris Spassky at the World Championships in Reykjavík in 1972 mirrored the Cold War tensions between the USA and the USSR. I longed to be a brilliant chess player and to find a variation that would astonish the chess world. So I spent days studying grandmasters old and new to see if I could guess their next move. I was introduced to the genius of Morphy, Alekhine, Lasker, Botvinnik, Tal and others. However, chess was extremely time-consuming, and although it had helped to while away the lonely holiday hours, it also ate into my study time. This was not helped by my competitive spirit: I was determined to become the local club champ. But the closest I got was a draw against the reigning club champ after three hours of play. This was not bad for a 16-year-old, but I wanted to do better.

My first love, however, was tennis. The Homes had three asphalt hard courts and my athleticism and height had made me the best player there. Again, I would hone my skills during the long holidays, practising my serves on the courts or volleying against the wall to improve my reactions and wrist strength. Uncle Mike and Auntie June were tennis fans, so we always watched Wimbledon. My hero was the Swede Björn Borg, who at that time swept all before him with his impeccable behaviour and heavily top-spun ground strokes. I would train hard to emulate him. While I was living with Mr and Mrs Masters I would cycle to the Homes to continue practising, even in darkness – all the better to improve my reactions! I started with a slightly luminous yellow foam tennis ball and then graduated to a real ball which would emerge out of the darkness at lightning speed. It was exhilarating to hit the ball cleanly several times in succession, and there were times when I wondered if I would make it as a professional. But by the summer of 1977 I realised that to make progress I would need a wealthy sponsor. Besides that, if I wasn't successful or suffered a career-ending injury, I would be left without qualifications or decent prospects. I reluctantly relinquished that dream to pursue the much safer option of exams, qualifications and a good job. But I nonetheless continued to spend more time on my hobbies than was good for me. This was certainly the view of Mr and Mrs Masters, although they didn't help matters by getting me a well-paid night job at a local theatre which took up even more of my free time. The theatre paid me the princely sum of 50p per hour, rising to 75p for unsocial hours – which were the hours I tended to work. Two or three hours of this work was equal to a six-day newspaper round wage, so it was very good money. I worked out that within months I would have enough to buy a brand-new top-of-the-range tennis racket and proper Borg-like shorts and tennis shoes. And to my delight (and Mr and Mrs Masters' disappointment) I was absolutely right!

When I was not practising my tennis in the dark, I was at the theatre helping with stage scenery, moving chairs, operating lights and keeping well away from wiring tasks! I would often work from 7pm to 11pm and sometimes until 1am. By the time I had cycled the four miles home it was typically after midnight before I was asleep. But burning the candle at both ends wasn't sustainable: I was putting my studies in jeopardy. And so it was just a matter of time before things came to a head.

Sometimes it is the little things rather than the larger things in life that bring about a crisis. One of those little things was Mr and Mrs Masters' neurotic dog. Every time it heard a noise outside the front door it would run up and down the entrance lobby barking loudly. It would continue the barking well after the noise − a pedestrian walking by, a loud car or motorcycle or another dog − had abated. The street was not unduly busy, but still the dog barked loudly and incessantly. Many was the time I would be deep in thought in my bedroom, only to be distracted by yet another neurotic canine tantrum erupting directly below me. It was impossible to concentrate for any length of time. Mr and Mrs Masters were powerless to stop it happening and just told me to cope as best I could. But I wasn't coping. I was getting behind in my studies. And I was becoming very worried.

Added to this was an incident at the theatre which really shook me. One night I was responsible for operating one of two large stage spotlights located in a gallery high above the rear of the theatre. The spotlights – or 'limes' as they are known – were large, powerful arc lights that were each housed in a heavy circular metal frame about 18 inches in diameter which slotted into a vertical metal tube-like stand enabling the lime to be raised and lowered as required. Once activated, the lime components producing the arc light became white hot and heated up the surrounding metal frame so that it was impossible to touch it without being badly burnt. The beam was directed at the stage by grasping two insulated handles either side of the circular metal frame. This was not usually problematic but, on this occasion, the electrician asked me to lean the lime slightly out of the gallery window and to the left to spotlight a local celebrity, who would enter the auditorium from the extreme right. This was a tricky manoeuvre, but I was assisted by a new lime operator called Pete. I was nervous about Pete since he admitted to being imprisoned for stabbing someone and I wasn't sure if I might be next! To cut a long story short, the lime almost fell out of the window onto the audience, and it was only Pete's quick thinking and bravery that prevented certain death and injury to those seated below. His courage and quick thinking averted a certain disaster. I was both amazed and grateful. I was also ashamed that I had judged him so severely. Yes, this man has stabbed another person, but he had also demonstrated tremendous courage and quick thinking in my moment of need. I had wrongly written him off as an ex-con who was to be kept at arm's length and not to be trusted. I now realised that he was an exceptionally brave man who had saved many lives that night. His bravery was never acknowledged because the story never got out. He shrugged it off as of no real consequence, but I was deeply marked by the incident and decided that I would resign from the job before anything else like that happened. I also resigned because I was not getting enough sleep, and this was adversely affecting my studies. Although I was reluctant to part with the cash, my fear of exam failure and the prospect of being stuck in a dead-end existence helped me make this decision.

I also decided that I needed a more conducive study environment and discussed my thoughts with John Honey, who realised that I needed immediate help. He offered me a place back at the Homes for the duration of my studies. The placement had lasted just five of the 18 months originally envisaged, but he had no hesitation in taking me back, and on 28th May I returned to the Homes under the care of Auntie Maureen, this time based in St David's (Block 2).

I immediately relaxed. It was like coming home again with everything and everyone so familiar. Maureen cared for me in a very relaxed and motherly way, and I got on particularly well with her teenage son, Peter, who happened to be about my equal at tennis. Although it was only a matter of days before my first exams, I threw myself into study with gusto. My teachers provided good revision tools and I studied day and night to make up lost ground.

Mr and Mrs Masters probably felt that they had failed me. But as John Honey stated in his letter of thanks to them dated 1st June: *Please do not feel you have failed in any way, it has in fact been a very good opportunity for David to have an insight into what he would eventually have to face when he leaves permanent care.* The whole point of the placement was to ease me out of institutional care and into the wider world in a carefully managed manner. This was all the more important to me, an only child, with no family home to go to and no relatives to support me in that process. As previously mentioned, Spurgeon's leavers did not necessarily have supportive parents, but in my case, I was clearly alone and had become 'institutionalised' during my 16 years at the Homes. I was thus a unique case and needed all the help I could get to make that transition. Mr and Mrs Masters were an important part of that process.

My exams came and went, and Peter and I enjoyed playing back-to-back tennis matches during the sun-drenched sweltering days that characterised the summer of 1977. We also celebrated the Queen's Silver Jubilee, but it was a bittersweet moment in that there were now so few children and staff to celebrate as the Homes wound down.

If tennis and chess were my main passions, then the Swedish supergroup ABBA came closely behind. I had used some of my theatre earnings to subscribe to the UK ABBA fan club and buy as many of their vinyl records as possible, some of which were original Swedish language versions. I was, of course (like so many other adoring male fans), particularly taken with the blonde lead singer Agnetha. The fact that she had married the rather ordinary looking Björn Ulvaeus gave me hope that there may be other blonde Swedish beauties out there who would find me attractive. I certainly felt that I was more handsome than Björn, although admittedly I didn't have the chiselled looks or athletic physique of that other

Swedish superstar, Björn Borg. But I reckoned that I ranked in looks somewhere between the two of them. So, when I read in the fan magazine that a 16-year-old Swedish girl wanted an English-speaking penfriend, I couldn't put pen to paper quickly enough. Her name was Lena and she lived in the southern Swedish town of Lund. We eventually swapped photos, with me trying as best I could to cover my embarrassing acne, and we arranged to meet while she was on an exchange trip to Wales during late July and early August.

But there was a problem. I was penniless! I had spent most of my theatre money on tennis equipment and ABBA paraphernalia and my only income was £1.50 weekly pocket money. This was certainly not enough to buy a tent, food, drink and return bus ticket, and then rent a patch on the campsite and entertain Lena. It seemed that my plan to secure a beautiful Swedish girlfriend was doomed from the start. John Honey came to the rescue once again, providing me with a paid part-time job at the Homes' stores, lending me a sleeping bag and finding a tent that I could borrow.

At the appointed time I travelled with the staff and children to their summer holiday destination in the village of Weston in the Northamptonshire countryside. From there I travelled on to the Welsh tourist resort of Colwyn Bay. I then introduced myself to the lead Swedish teacher, a thirty-something blonde and bearded fun-loving man called Arne. He received me warmly and introduced me to the whole group and included me in their itinerary as a guest. The romance with Lena sadly lasted just a few days.

The weather also failed to live up to expectations. The camp site was a field at Ty Ucha Farm on the outskirts of Colwyn Bay, and the first few nights were uneventful. But inevitably it poured down one night and continued to do so for the next couple of days. It was then, and only then, that I learned that my tent was in fact a *toy* children's tent meant for dry-weather play. It had neither waterproofing nor strength. So, during the night the rain penetrated the tent walls and roof and my belongings and my sleeping bag became soaked through. My tent was also completely saturated, but the two wooden guideposts seemed strong enough to bear the additional weight until during one memorable night I heard an ominous 'Crack!' as the post at the entrance broke in two and the front of the tent collapsed on me. I was able to reconnect the broken pieces, but the upper piece leant precariously outwards at an angle of about 45 degrees. It would only take another downpour or strong gust of wind to bring it down again. Which is precisely what happened. I managed to eke out my money for the whole two weeks thanks to Arne's hospitality, but by the final Sunday I was glad to be on the bus returning to Weston.

It had been my first independent expedition ever, and it had taught me some very important lessons about life. The most important of these was to accept help in time of need when it is genuinely offered without feeling embarrassed or obliged to return the favour. Up to this point, and indeed throughout my time at the Homes, I had been in continual need and received help of every description. As I grew older and particularly during my teens this became a source of embarrassment to me:

I found it impossible to accept help or gifts because it reinforced my sense of low self-worth. What the 'holiday' in Wales taught me was that people were happy to help me because I needed help and not because they felt sorry for me as a child in care. But later and to my cost I didn't always remember this.

Chapter 11

U-turn

I returned to Weston for two weeks with the children and staff of the Homes. The weather throughout was a very sunny and pleasant contrast to the Welsh rain. We were guests of the members of Weston Baptist Chapel who allowed us to use their hall to sleep, eat and relax in. We had a very full itinerary of sightseeing, picnics, games and farm-related activities such as baling hay and feeding the animals. Our hosts invited us to their homes for meals and to their gardens for picnics, barbecues and delicious teas, and made our stay an absolute pleasure.

But the even deeper impact they made on me prompted me to ask two questions: 'Why are these people so kind to us without expecting anything back?' and: 'What *exactly* is it that they have got, that I don't have but I'm drawn to?' This was the first time I had really noticed an attractiveness in Christians. There were some exceptions of course, but in general my experience up to that point was of rather earnest but dull people whose main concern was whether they would make it to heaven. The Weston Christians, by contrast, found joy in the here and now and in each other's company. The chapel services were full of laughter, testimonies, and modern songs and instruments.

I was particularly struck one Sunday by the testimonies of a group of young people who were due to start university and were being baptised. They talked easily and naturally about how real God was to them and how they had found faith. Then each of them entered the baptistery and were immersed under the water, emerging joyful and radiant. It was hard for anyone not to be moved by this, and to my surprise and then horror I found myself struggling to contain huge waves of emotion. Thankfully, I had taken the precaution of sitting in the rear balcony away from most of the congregation. This was just as well because I then began to weep uncontrollably. I punched myself hard in the ribs and midriff several times but was unable to stop, although I was able to stifle the loudest of my sobs. To my relief no one from the ground floor looked up at me and eventually the service ended.

As soon as the minister, Alan Payne, said the final 'Amen', I rushed towards the balcony stairs to be first out of the building so that no one would notice my embarrassing emotional state. I hoped to find a convenient private spot where I could then recover myself. But as I hastily made my way to the one and only staircase in the corner, a little old lady appeared out of nowhere, blocked my path and, putting her hand on my forearm, asked, 'Young man, do you want to give your life to Christ?' Her intended meaning was clearly: 'Young man, you *do* want to, don't you?' My reaction was immediate and decisive: 'No, not today! Not today!' As I tried to contain those powerful and confusing emotions I threw my arm up, releasing her grip, and ran down the stairs as fast as my legs would carry me. I eventually found a secluded spot where I was able to calm down and reappear without anyone knowing what I'd experienced.

The whole episode had been profoundly embarrassing. More than that, the baptisms had triggered shockingly powerful emotions that left me bewildered and confused. I needed answers, but who could I ask? I needed someone relatively anonymous, but who was likely to understand what had happened to me. I decided I would ask Alan Payne and turned up unannounced the next morning at the manse. Alan and Lynn were a young couple in their late 20s and had steadily built up the congregation of what was their first ministry posting. Their warm and gentle character made them very approachable, and I soon found myself pouring out my story to Alan over a mug of tea while seated at his kitchen table. He listened intently and sympathetically for a while, and then I asked, 'What does it all mean?' He answered: 'It is God showing you how much he loves you.' This was a completely new concept for me, and I asked him to explain. I don't remember all that he said as he explained the Christian gospel. But I do remember him clearly setting out what Jesus Christ had done for me and what he offered me in a way that I had not understood before. 'Of course I was a sinner!' There was no denying that: I hadn't even lived up to my own modest standards, let alone God's! Of course I needed and wanted forgiveness, and if God was willing to give it, then I would accept it. But did I want to follow Jesus – to trust him in everything? Yes I did, and even without knowing all that that would entail, I had heard enough from Alan and seen enough in the Weston Christians to want to take that step of faith. Somehow Alan made the Christian life sound both serious *and* exciting, so I agreed there and then to follow him in a prayer of commitment. When we finished I knew that my sins had been forgiven and that somehow something important had changed.

It is very unlikely that during all those years of churchgoing and Christian input at the Homes that no one had explained the Christian gospel (good news) clearly to me. What makes most sense to me is that those two days in the summer of 1977 were what may be termed 'divine appointments'. The Bible writers speak of time in (roughly) two ways: as Chronos (chronological time) and Kairos (God's opportune time). That Sunday and Monday were my Kairos moments when my heart reached out to God and God reached out to me. It was real and it was life changing. For me, the best comparison is as follows: it was like visiting a chiropractor and hearing the 'click' of misaligned bones being put back into place, followed by a new freedom of movement and sense of well-being throughout the whole body as other joints, tendons, ligaments and muscles begin to function more effectively. This is how it was with my conversion. The Spirit of God had, with my consent and cooperation, re-orientated the very core of my being towards my Maker, and the rest of me began to move into alignment, albeit slowly and sometimes imperceptibly, with that fundamental shift.

Alan had told me that it was important to tell someone about my decision as soon as possible, so on returning to the Homes I sought out Maureen and Peter because I knew they were Christians. I had been to Peter's baptism and knew they would understand what I'd done and why. I was somewhat afraid of being misunderstood and ridiculed by others, but thankfully that didn't happen. Besides, events were moving very quickly, and I had other vitally important matters to attend to.

The first of these was what would happen when I reached the age of 18, now less than four months away. At that point the Homes would no longer have legal responsibility for my care, and I would have to leave.

I had thought long and hard over the previous 18 months about what I would do. My dominant emotion was dread of the unknown, a deep-seated fear that, once beyond the safety and familiarity of all that had been my life up to that point, I would fall into a bottomless chasm of nothingness. I had had noble thoughts of putting aside my educational aspirations to care for my patently needy mother on leaving the Homes. My meeting with her in 1975 and the shock I had felt at her physical demeanour and evident mental anguish had left me with a very strong sense of duty to care for her. In fact, I told June Shearn that this is what I intended to do. June's response was full of wisdom, and it saved me from myself. She listened sympathetically, with real concern for both my mother and me, and then looked very lovingly and earnestly at me as she said: 'David, you have to think of yourself and how you are going to make your way in the world.' She clearly saw that I needed to make the most of the limited opportunities I had, before having any realistic hope of helping my mother. There was no question that my mother was so seriously ill that I would be incapable of caring for her even if I wanted to. I realised that June was absolutely right, and her wise words helped me focus on making the best of my abilities.

However, by August 1977 I still didn't know what I was going to do because I still didn't know if I'd passed enough exams to allow me to move on to A-levels. Eventually the dreaded day came and the news that awaited me was mixed: I had failed one of my exams outright and marginally failed two others. But the good news was that I had passed five exams which, along with my three CSE grade 1s, meant that I could proceed to A-levels! These results were a vindication of my exam strategy. I had felt very unprepared on returning to the Homes that May, and so I had focused on just six of the eight subjects. These positive results now gave me the confidence to test my ability at A-level. But where precisely was I going to study and, more importantly, where was I going to live?

At this point, John Honey amazed me by asking how I would feel about moving to Coventry and living with Mike and June from September to December. I would be one of the first to live in a newly acquired house purchased by the Homes in accordance with the new policy of smaller care units for children. I could then begin working for my A-levels at The Butts Technical College and, when I turned 18 at the end of the year, the Homes would help find me private accommodation and pay me a weekly allowance to enable me to complete my studies.

Even as I write these words I'm staggered by the generosity of this offer, which had been conceived by John Honey and whole-heartedly endorsed by the Board of Trustees. But much more importantly, this offer was an endorsement of *me*. It was a vote of real confidence in *me* to succeed in the face of not inconsiderable difficulties. And so, I was off to Coventry.

But it proved to be the hardest time of my life.

Chapter 12

Struggling – Really Struggling

Mike and June gave me a soft landing in Coventry. We knew each other well and it was easy to adjust to the homely new surroundings at Earlsdon Avenue in the southern suburb of Earlsdon. The six-bedroom house had been bought by the Homes from a successful solicitor and it showed. There were leaded diamond-shaped windows, wooden floors and oak panels. It was a beautiful house, and it's easy to see why childcare experts preferred smaller scale units such as this. I had my own bedroom, and there were very few other children at that time to disturb me as I adjusted to life outside 'the Homes'.

Those adjustments proved to be numerous, substantial and, at times, overwhelming. My first task was to enrol at the nearby Butts Technical College to study for geography, history and English A-levels. What struck me was just how few lectures were timetabled compared with Dane Court and how much self-discipline was expected of me. My fellow students were friendly enough, but I was understandably evasive when responding to questions about my family, where I lived and how I came to be in Coventry. I was afraid that they would ridicule, shun or patronise me because of my background. So for the four months I was at Earlsdon Avenue I avoided making close friends and simply focused on my studies.

I was desperate to be accepted by my lecturers and fellow students. If I didn't feel I could be accepted by revealing who I really was, i.e. a child in care, then I could at least hope to be accepted as a capable student. The Spurgeon's Trustees certainly gave me the tools to do that. They paid for all my books and stationery together with the course and examination fees. So I was not at a disadvantage in that respect. Without that support I simply could not have begun to study because there were always too few course books in the college library for all of us to borrow. Buying our own copies was therefore essential – but very expensive.

It was also essential for me to move into my own accommodation. So, on 14th January 1978 I moved into a small, three-bedroom terraced house in Mayfield Road, just a five-minute walk from the Earlsdon Avenue property. I shared the house with two men in their mid-20s, Pete and Chris.

My first impressions were that the property was basic and small (it was), and the same was true of my bedroom. It consisted of a chest of drawers, a wardrobe, a bookcase, a bed, a bedside cabinet and a gas fire activated by a coin meter. The synthetic carpet was dark purple and the curtains were a faded brown. The walls were painted magnolia and the woodwork white. A shared bathroom was immediately adjacent. This was, in summary, a small, no-frills house for rent at the cheap end of the market. I remember thinking as I moved in, 'This is *so* different to what I'm used to!' But I realised that I had no choice but to accept the inevitable. There was, however, one redeeming feature that I definitely appreciated: it was only a short walk from Mike and June should I need support or a change of scenery.

But it *was* small. Not that I possessed many belongings, but mentally, that took some getting used to. So, I unpacked my small suitcase, plugged in my portable record player and placed my tennis rackets against the wardrobe side. I remember sitting on the edge of the bed that first evening with my hands in my lap feeling terribly homesick and thinking, 'You're on your own now. It's up to you to make the most of your circumstances and opportunities.' In fact, I was not completely on my own. But it *felt* that way. What *was* true was that no one could study or achieve good exam results for me. That was ultimately my responsibility. I knew that, and it weighed on me very heavily.

I paid rent of £12.50 per week and about £2.50 for gas and electricity. With what I received from the Trustees, there was £5 left over to spend on food, clothing and leisure activities. The Trustees were under no obligation at all to pay this allowance, but it soon became clear to me that this was not enough on which to live. Chris, who worked for the Social Security Department, told me that if applied for state benefits as a student I would get at least £30 per week and my rent paid. I would have been much better off on state benefits, but I didn't take Chris's advice because I was daunted by the unfamiliar bureaucracy of the benefits system, and also feared that by putting myself at the mercy of the state and accepting benefits, I would then lose the Trustees' lifeline forever. So I slowly but surely got further and further into debt.

In retrospect, the Trustees substantially underestimated my living costs and unwittingly exposed me to unnecessary financial pressure. When I was living with Mr and Mrs Masters, the Trustees provided a weekly allowance for my care of £15 per week which did not include rent (£12.50). On this basis I should have been offered £32.50 per week rather than £20, so no wonder I struggled! But I felt too proud to ask for more.

Initially, I managed my debt by arranging a bank overdraft, but this simply got larger and larger. I then started defaulting on my payments to the landlady so I tried to reduce my heating and food costs to compensate. I spent less and less time in my cold bedroom to avoid feeding the gas meter with coins, and more time in the communal sitting room and even more in the city reference library which stayed open until 10pm. The main thing was that the library was warm. When I returned to the cold house, I boiled the kettle and filled three or four old glass soft-drink bottles to place in the bed. I couldn't really afford a proper hot water bottle, so I made do with these. They occasionally leaked and always eventually made their way to the side or the bottom of the bed where they made a gentle clinking sound during the night. But they did stay warm long enough to get me off to sleep.

My diet was becoming very restricted as I cut my food costs. I was increasingly living on chips, pancakes of various kinds, jacket potatoes, milk, yogurt and eggs. I couldn't afford fruit or vegetables . . . but I could afford beans on toast.

Beans, I had learnt, were a cheap protein source, so on one memorable occasion I took myself off to the local Sainsbury's supermarket where beans were on offer. Sensing the opportunity to make a big saving I filled my trolley with 20 or so of the tins and joined the checkout queue amongst the 'normal' trolleys of food. I put the tins of beans in rows of two on the conveyor belt until all 20 lay there with no other food items. The cashier looked at me and then looked at the beans and then back at me with a mixture of bewilderment and concern before saying, 'Are you *alright*, dear?' 'Yes,' I replied, 'I'm just poor.' She seemed satisfied with my reply and helped me stack the tins into two carrier bags. I ate lots of beans on toast over the next two weeks and still love them!

But these measures simply couldn't offset the gap between my income and expenditure and so I fell further and further into debt. During the winter, I would often gaze at the flickering gas fire and ponder whether to feed the meter another ten-pence piece to keep my room warm for another hour or two or hold it back for food. I grew to appreciate first-hand how people in debt feel. I oscillated between denial that this wasn't *really* happening to me, and gnawing anxiety that I was *never* going to get out of this mess. I would lie awake during the long hours of the night and sit drowsily in lectures thinking constantly of the hopelessness of it all. The debt weighed heavily on every aspect of my life. Sleep became a welcome escape but when I awoke the heaviness returned. I simply couldn't shake it off. Eventually things came to a head when the landlady's patience ran out and she asked me to pay all my arrears by the end of the year. Of course, I was unable to pay and so I reluctantly approached John Honey for help: his letter to me dated 31st January 1979 says it all.

Dear David,

Further to your request for financial help, I've spoken to the Trustees and am pleased to tell you that for this occasion they are prepared to make you an allowance of £37. However, I must stress that they are deeply concerned that you do not run yourself into debt again and would like to have some assurance as to how your payments can be made regularly to your landlady. We would not wish to undermine your responsibility in this matter by paying the rent on your behalf. Would you, therefore, let me know exactly how you intend to overcome this difficulty. We obviously do want to help you in any way that we can, and I would stress how much I appreciate the fact that you made a direct approach to me in this matter. Incidentally what is your rent and how do you allocate your £20 weekly allowance? If you have any difficulty in cashing the enclosed cheque or paying it into your Post Office account, please let me know.

The *allowance of £37* was not an increase in my weekly allowance, but an increase to enable me to pay off the rent arrears. As such, it merely postponed rather than resolved my financial difficulties which continued to cause me a great deal of stress and substantially reduced my quality of life. But I nonetheless felt a great sense of relief to be free from the immediate pressure. Once again, I had John Honey and the Trustees to thank for this.

But there was another burden of a non-financial kind that they could not share, and it was to make its presence felt during the following 12 months.

In the meantime, I regularly played tennis at the nearby Spencer Park tennis courts, which were free of charge, and became an honorary member of a civil servants' tennis club. I also enjoyed borrowing classical music tapes and vinyl records from the city library at no charge, furthering my interest in classical music that had been encouraged by Mike Shearn. I particularly enjoyed Verdi's music as well as the popular classics by Grieg, Dvořák, Beethoven, Mozart and Bach.

Despite my straitened financial circumstances, and on the advice of the staff of a nearby independent record shop, I purchased five LPs that became especially important to me and to my mental health. They came to resonate emotionally with me during good times and bad, which I found incredibly comforting. The five were Grieg's Piano Concerto in A Major with Peer Gynt on side B; Dvořák's New World Symphony and Piano Quintet in A Major; Beethoven's Emperor Concerto; Holst's The Planets Suite; and, my absolute favourite, Rachmaninoff's Piano Concerto No.2 in C Minor. These were my emotional companions and empathisers during the year of 1979, probably the most difficult year of my entire life.

I had an additional motive for buying the LPs, and it had to do with a girl who was studying at the Coventry School of Music. I wanted to impress her with at least some understanding of her chosen subject. Not that the relationship ever got off the ground, because I mistook her liking for me for much more than that. And, in any case, how was I ever going to answer the inevitable questions that her nice middle-class parents would ask me about my own parents and prospects, even assuming I were ever introduced? No, it was a nice thought but just an illusion.

Chapter 13

False Friends and True Friends

But at least I was starting to make friends. Among these was a Scouser called Bernard who was the most accepting of me. He introduced me to the delights of politics, and I struck up a good friendship with Andy M, his avowedly Marxist politics lecturer. We met with other interested students and lecturers in The Albany, a smoke-filled pub close to the college, to discuss all the subjects that are usually taboo in polite company, namely politics, religion and sex. It was a bit of an education for me, and I initially just listened, accepted the free drinks and enjoyed the stimulating company and soon realised that I was completely out of my depth. Nonetheless, the group made me feel included and I warmed to that. I found these informal meetings intellectually stimulating and felt challenged to get myself mentally fit enough to participate fully and to defend my opinions and beliefs. In particular, I felt the need to defend my Christian faith in the face of stridently expressed atheistic beliefs and others' scepticism of anything that could be termed 'truth', religious or otherwise.

There were a number of Christian books that I found particularly helpful at the time, including Michael Green's popular apologetic paperback *You Must Be Joking!* and Dr James Dobson's book on male-female relationships, *Man-To-Man About Women*. I also appreciated R.C. Sproul's *The Psychology of Atheism*, which had a more academic approach and made the point that if religious belief met a deep-seated psychological need to believe in God as many atheists claimed, then it might also be the case that atheism met a psychological need *not* to believe in God. These books didn't provide anything like adequate refutations of the arguments I was facing, but they did enable me to organise my thoughts in helpful ways, assuring me that despite my feelings of intellectual inferiority, there were academically and pastorally qualified Christians who could very capably defend beliefs similar to my own.

This realisation was very important to me because I found the pub discussions raising all kinds of fundamental issues about knowledge, truth, identity, purpose, human relationships, reality and values. The Greek philosopher Socrates said that the unexamined life is not worth living, and I whole-heartedly agreed. Avoiding these fundamental and complex issues was not something I was prepared to do, no matter how ill-equipped I felt in the face of very powerful and plausible challenges to what I'd been taught to believe. For example, I was taught from an early age that there *is* such a thing as right and wrong and I took this for granted. But as I grew older, I began to question this and other assumptions, and for this I am thankful for Mike Shearn's encouragement to be curious and explore issues in a genuine spirit of enquiry. I recall one memorable occasion at King Eths when my friends and I had taken pleasure in bullying a girl about some now-forgotten matter. At first I joined them in their mocking laughter but then on seeing the girl's tears I felt deeply ashamed of myself, and that prompted the questions, 'Why do I feel that this is wrong?' and 'What exactly is wrong and right?' Now just a few years later, I was being challenged again to provide satisfactory answers to similar questions. And as it happened, my lecturers were not the only ones seeking to influence my thinking and to befriend me.

Leaving the city library for home one night, I was approached on the street by a pleasant-mannered young man in his 20s who engaged me in conversation about the meaning of life. Andreas was an Austrian working for an organisation called the Unification Church, which was seeking to unify all Christians into one Church. That idea appealed to me, so I accepted his invitation to a meeting a few days later with other like-minded young people. The food and friendship were good (and free!), and I happily accepted a further invitation to a weekend meeting in Swansea at which I was introduced to an even larger group. Andreas and his friends were very affirming, and they encouraged me to ask as many questions as I liked. I seemed to be among kindred spirits, and I readily agreed to spend a week at the Church's London headquarters at Lancaster Gate near Hyde Park.

Apart from the three mealtimes, the days consisted of a mixture of recreational activities in Hyde Park and teaching sessions at the headquarters which were conducted by one of the leaders named John, a former headteacher who seemed intellectually very able. My group was made up of about 20 men and women in our late teens and early 20s who were all earnestly seeking answers to the fundamental questions I was asking, and Andreas and John encouraged us to ask such questions and to share our hopes and dreams. Andreas told me that this week was a time of 'getting to know us', and I could get to know more about the Unification Church by going on an all-expenses-paid month-long residential course held in a large manor house in the English countryside. It sounded very attractive, but by this time I was becoming suspicious.

Although I enjoyed the camaraderie, I noticed that quite a few members of the group were running away from difficult situations such as broken relationships, violent home lives, drug addictions and loneliness (I put myself in the latter category).

It also struck me that those providing hospitality for us all seemed to be foreign and hence dislocated from their home countries. They also worked extraordinarily long hours in return for just board and lodging. They didn't seem to have a life outside the headquarters: in fact, there was a very heavy security presence at the main entrance monitoring comings and goings. By contrast, people like Andreas had much more freedom and seemed to enjoy greater material benefits. I remember overhearing Andreas telling another person that he would be buying his brother a saxophone for his birthday: this concerned me because I had been told that Church members worked for free and gave all their money and possessions to the Church when they joined permanently. This seemed to be a double standard, and it aroused my suspicions. I began to view the Church and its recruiters with much more critical eyes, and my suspicions were finally confirmed during one of the teaching sessions with John.

He started with a broad and convincing sweep of human origins and history, together with a diagnosis of what had gone wrong with the world. It seemed broadly consistent with Christian teaching until he got to the crucifixion and resurrection. He told us that, contrary to orthodox Christian teaching, Jesus Christ had failed in his mission to redeem humanity from sin and its consequences, and that therefore a second Saviour was required to complete this task – the so-called 'Lord of the Second Advent'. Despite being pressed, neither John nor Andreas would tell us who this person was, saying it was for us to decide. But it gradually became clear that this person was to be identified with a Korean man called Rev. Sun Myung Moon. More than that, Rev. Moon had written a divinely inspired book, *The Divine Principle,* which superseded the Bible. Putting all my observations together with my admittedly rudimentary Bible knowledge, I realised that there was something badly wrong with this organisation, so I started to ask more searching questions. I eventually concluded that the Unification Church, also known as 'The Moonies', was a cult. They would use psychological techniques to control adherents, and geographical relocation to loosen and sever family ties. I was to learn that very few people who embarked on the one-month workshop at the country house failed to become members. But by the end of the first week at the headquarters I saw the danger signs, and decided to tag along in Coventry so that I could covertly dissuade others from joining.

I kept this up for about six months, after which it was made very clear to me that I was no longer welcome. I could see how emotionally vulnerable people, especially young adults, could be sucked into this cult and then find it impossible to leave. In the end, I believe that my attempts to help others see the dangers had limited success. In some ways it had been a close call for me and a salutary reminder that I was not the only vulnerable person looking for answers.

I was having to learn fast and although I occasionally attended a large local Baptist church I didn't feel that I was getting the answers I needed. These issues were not usually addressed in a way that would help me hold my own in the pub, or with the likes of Andreas and John.

There was, however, one person at the church who did seem to understand what I was driving at, and seeing how pastorally needy I was, she reached out to me. I will call her Sarah and she was several years older than me, becoming at that time something like an older sister. She was one of the driving and organising forces within the young people's group and she was concerned that I was setting impossibly high expectations for myself. I remember her asking me during 1978 what kind of grades I expected to get. My reply was that I couldn't allow myself to think of getting less than straight A's. Her very concerned response was, 'But what if you don't get straight A's? Then what are your plans?', to which I replied, 'I can't afford to think like that.' It was clear that a new fear of failure was driving my thoughts and behaviour towards dangerous perfectionism and destructive black-and-white thinking. This perfectionism was my way of denying the possibility of failure, and that was what triggered Sarah's concern for me.

There was some basis for my rigid optimism, as my lecturers expected me to achieve A's or B's. So once John

Honey had assured me of continuing financial support to cover such items as holiday accommodation and living expenses, I applied for university places. I chose all the top-ranked universities except Oxford and Cambridge, on the grounds that I was better off being at the top of the second division than the bottom of the first. My feeling was that at Oxbridge I would have neither the money nor the social skills to integrate with my wealthy peers. The London School of Economics was the only university which offered me a place, and that was on condition that I achieved two A's and a B. The bar was thus placed very high. Still, I had an offer: the Trustees paid the £25 Hall of Residence deposit and on 29th June John Honey confirmed to me that the Trustees *will supplement your allowance to meet your general requirements*, including a book allowance and finance for holiday-time accommodation and living expenses. So far, so good.

But only four days later I wrote to John, feeling anything but confident about my exam results. I knew that I had not answered all the questions in any of my exams and was starting to fear the worst. I explained to John that *I might very well fail this year . . . Would it be possible for me, with your help, to retake my exams in January 1980? I would then propose to get a full-time job until the October, when I would definitely take a degree of some description.* Perhaps Sarah's advice to make contingency plans was starting to sink in . . . In any case, I would not get my results until late August and spent the summer working for the City Council as a casual gardener.

When they came, my results were not at all good. I had failed one subject completely and received an unclassified and an E in the other two. And this from a student who was predicted to achieve A's and B's! It was one thing for me to *suspect* that I had performed badly at my exams; it was quite another to face the appalling reality and the dreadful consequences. My dream of attending the London School of Economics had gone for good. I was now faced with the nightmare of resits and, even worse, another year in debt and living at Mayfield Road.

Despite this, John Honey found some encouraging words to say. In a letter dated 18th September he wrote: *Congratulations on your passes and I'm sure you will eventually make university with your obvious determination.* I was indeed still determined: after all, the alternatives to success were for me unthinkable. I simply *had* to pass my exams.

I had fallen in love with politics, so I decided to add that to the other three A-levels which I would take in the new academic year. I paid the £183 exam fees for two of these from my summer job income, with the Trustees paying for the other two. In addition, the Trustees agreed to cover the cost of new books and to increase my weekly allowance to £27.50 from October. Although this was an improvement, it was still insufficient for my needs, despite John Honey's assurance, *If, for any reason, you feel this does not cover your expenses at any time, please let me know,* I felt too embarrassed to ask for more. This was another instance of my long history of *needing* the help of others, but not being able to fully *admit* it and to *accept* that help with good grace. It was my attempt to salvage at least some self-respect and to maintain the illusion that I was not completely dependent on others. But both the premise and conclusion of my reasoning were faulty. The Trustees' help was not in any way intended to diminish me as a person; rather, it was freely offered to enable me to reach my true potential. There is nothing noble about being poor or in need, and nothing shameful about accepting the help of others offered as an expression of their love and care. I may have *felt* indebted to the Trustees and thereby diminished, but the truth was that their generosity flowed from a genuine desire to help me with absolutely no conditions attached. The problem was mine and not theirs. But at the time, all I felt was a sense of obligation and shame, compounded by my exam failures. I masked this outwardly in my letters that indicated that I was *enjoying my studies* because I was now more familiar with the subjects. But the mask didn't stay on for very long.

Chapter 14

The Two Letters

The winter of 1979 was drawing near and that meant darker nights, colder weather, larger fuel bills and more financial pressure. To cap it all, my bedroom roof had sprung a leak, so every time it rained, water would drip through my plaster ceiling and into the empty plastic yoghurt pots I had scattered across the floor. I knew for certain that if I reported this to the landlady, all our rents would rise to cover the repair costs, and I couldn't risk that. So I had to live with a constant dripping which would fill the containers to overflowing and disturb my sleep. My circumstances were going from bad to worse.

I was also feeling the loss of former college friends who had now moved to universities without me. What remained unchanged were my lecturers and Bernard who had got himself elected as the full-time salaried student union president. But at almost 20 years of age, I was now two years older than my peers and I felt a bit of an outsider. All of this fed into my sense of failure and added to the unremitting pressure to succeed.

During my time in Coventry, I had maintained the link with my mother just to keep her up-to-date and to maintain contact with her social worker. I was by now an adult and, as her next of kin, I was frequently consulted by the Mental Health Tribunal before significant decisions were taken about her care or responses were made to any of my mother's complaints and requests. On one memorable occasion I had, with a large bouquet in hand, travelled the considerable distance to St Augustine's Hospital to visit her on Mother's Day. But I was turned away at the hospital reception on the grounds that she was too unwell to see me. The receptionist explained that my mother thought I was Michael Parkinson (a well-known television interviewer) and would appear with television cameras and bright lights to broadcast embarrassing pictures of her to millions of viewers. I was thoroughly upset by this, partly because of my wasted costly effort and partly because of her precarious mental state. So I decided not to visit again until I could be sure she was well enough to see me.

To be frank, I had more than enough to deal with that November without having to cope with my mother, and so I wasn't concerned that she hadn't written for some time. Then one evening I arrived home late to find a letter addressed to me in unfamiliar handwriting. I was intrigued and immediately took it to my room to read it.

I wish I hadn't. The letter was from the man my mother believed to be her father. I say 'believed' because there was some doubt about this. In any case, I had never met him nor had any contact with him whatsoever. He wrote that he had recently received a letter from my mother, in which she told him that I'd got a young woman pregnant at a party, and he proceeded to reprimand me in no uncertain terms. I was at my lowest ebb, and this was just too much to take. I was struggling with mounting debt, recent exam failure and feelings of loneliness. The combined psychological pressure of these things was a crushing burden. Now someone I had never met and who had never previously communicated with me was severely chastising me for something I had not done. The initial sensations of shock and disbelief soon turned to anger – anger directed not so much at this unknown man, but at my mother who had caused him to write the letter in the first place. I had had enough! I sat down to write my own and final letter to my troublesome mother.

It was as if the letter I'd received had triggered a whole range of dormant but powerful emotions and thoughts that I had managed to keep suppressed over the years. But now they erupted and found expression in my letter, the gist of which was that this was the last straw; neither of my parents had done anything for me and neither they nor any of my relatives had been there for me when I needed them. Where had they been? Did they care? As far as I was concerned, my mother was no longer my mother, and my relatives were no longer my relatives. I disowned her and them from this point on and didn't want any more contact with any of them. I was so angry that if I could have written the letter in my own blood, then I would have done so. But as it was, I just wanted to vent my anger and take it out on my mother.

When we are in so much pain, we sometimes attempt to completely cut ourselves off from the sources of that pain. This letter was intended to cut me off permanently from my mother and relatives, and I scrabbled around my room for an envelope and a first-class stamp – I wanted her to get this as soon as possible! I flew down the stairs, rushed out of the front door and turned left out of the gate.

It was raining and it was dark. I slowed as I approached the nearby bright-red cast-iron post box. I put the envelope into the mouth of the box and let it rest there. Once it was gone, it was gone, and I wouldn't be able to retrieve it. I knew precisely what impact this would have on my mother: it would be absolutely devastating. Her social worker had told me that I was probably the only positive thing in her life. She barely had any sense of self-worth, and this would almost certainly decimate what little remained.

I don't know precisely how long I stood there with the letter resting in the mouth of the box. It may have been a couple of minutes or as many as twenty. During such times of great stress time can appear to stand still. But however long I did in fact stand there in the rain and the darkness I eventually decided that I couldn't do that to my mother. I was less concerned for my relatives: they had their own lives and would cope irrespective of what I wrote about them. But my mother had only me. And so, I slowly – even reluctantly – withdrew the letter, ran all the way home, rattled up the staircase and threw myself onto the threadbare floor where I wept profusely until I could weep no more. Gradually I came to realise that this wasn't just about my mother; this was also about my current difficulties and the exam failures that threatened my future well-being.

I cried out to God in despair, 'What *is* my life about? If this is what my life amounts to, then it is just some kind of sick joke! I wish I had never been born!' I considered the option of suicide, but soon concluded that that would not really solve anything, and that I needed to face my pain and my fears and move on from them. Despite it all I actually wanted to live but I felt completely unloved and unlovable.

What happened next is very difficult to put into words. While I was contemplating ending it all, these words came into my mind: 'I love you . . . I always have . . . and I always will.' It was almost like a voice in my head speaking to me. This was so unexpected yet at the same time so real. I decided that although I was experiencing severe emotional pain, I wasn't having a psychotic episode. The words took me completely by surprise, and I decided that if they were from God and they were for me then I needed confirmation. I picked up my two-month-old New International Version (NIV) Bible and it fell open at Psalm 139. The verses that stood out to me were the following:

> *For you created my inmost being; you knit me together in my mother's womb ... your eyes saw my unformed body. All the days ordained for me were written in your book before one of them came to be.[1]*

I realised at that moment that I had a clear choice: I could choose to explain away this 'coincidence', or I could choose to give God the benefit of my very considerable doubt: that despite everything I was facing and despite everything I felt about myself, I could choose to believe that I was precious to God and that he had a purpose for my life. Or not.

I chose to believe that God did indeed have a purpose for my life and that if I could make something of my life, then in future years what I had experienced might give hope to others in similar circumstances. I don't know if I prayed at that point or not, but I do know that that same night I wrote another letter filled with emotion. A different letter. And to a different person.

On leaving the Homes I had been given my father's last known address in Switzerland. I now hurriedly scribbled that address onto an envelope, wrote two sentences on the writing paper before signing it and inserting it into the envelope. The next morning, I again turned left out of the front door and headed for the same bright-red cast-iron letterbox. This time I did not hesitate to post the letter. Its contents were very short: in addition to the date and my address, there were just two sentences:

Your son is weeping. Your son is weeping.

Chapter 15

Up and Out

My circumstances did not change at all that November night, but I felt I had new reasons for hope. By this time, I had become very introspective. In some ways the privacy of my own mind was a welcome solace and protection from my dreadful circumstances. It was probably because of those circumstances, along with my naturally enquiring mind, that I was more prone to introspection than others. I frequently engaged in internal dialogues triggered by insecurity along the lines of: 'What if . . . If only . . . On the one hand . . . But on the other . . .' I was continually hopping from one imponderable to another – trying to resolve the unresolvable and focusing inwards and downwards. To say that I was overthinking things would be an understatement!

I was pursuing the dangerous path of over-analysing my emotions and thoughts. 'Why do I feel anxious? Then, 'Why am I asking, "why do I feel anxious?"'. 'Why am I asking, "why am I asking, 'why do I feel x?'"' This infinite regression led me to very deep and unhelpful introspection. But I was alert to the danger, and frequently repeated to myself a little saying I had devised: 'I must rise up from the deepest.' I was aware that, emotionally speaking, unless I made a deliberate effort to keep my head above water, I would sink very easily and very quickly. Three things helped me rise up and out of this introspective abyss: music, the Bible and Spurgeon's staff.

Music often had a way of transporting me into a world that was a welcome distraction from my real-world concerns. When the others were out at work I could for example immerse myself into La Bohème or La Traviata and sing my heart out with the leading tenors until the dramatic finale. This form of emotional catharsis lifted my spirits at a time when I used to go to bed and close my eyes just to escape the reality of my life and to try to keep warm during the cold days and nights. On my worst days, and especially following my exam failure, I would repeatedly listen to the mournful strains of Grieg's 'Solveig's Song' and Holst's 'Saturn' (The Bringer of Old Age) and 'Neptune' (The Mystic). In a strange kind of way, I felt that Grieg and Holst had also lived through my experiences. But my greatest companion at that time was Rachmaninoff. If I needed some deep emotional catharsis then I would repeatedly play the slow second movement of the second piano concerto, wallowing in the pathos of its minor key. And at my absolute lowest, I would sneak into Chris's room while he was at work and play the record on his system to get the maximum effect of his enormous stereo speakers. This music connected with me emotionally in a way nothing else could. I felt understood and therefore not alone. I was particularly encouraged to read the record sleeve notes describing Rachmaninoff's descent into depression after the critical review of his first symphony, followed by his emergence to write his second piano concerto which confirmed his recovery and his genius. I was never clinically depressed, but his music mirrored my mood at that time, and I found great comfort in that.

I also found great comfort in the Bible. There is plenty in its pages to resonate with someone like me who felt lonely and abandoned by his family. Psalm 27:10 says: *Though my father and mother forsake me, the LORD will receive me.* In fact, the whole psalm is a cry for deliverance and a statement of confidence in God's ability to rescue those of us in distress. The psalms as a whole are a treasure trove of spiritual truth and emotional comfort. As I read through them, I found great reassurance that whatever my circumstances and feelings, God's love and concern for me remained undiminished.

At that time, John, Mike, June and Maureen were the physical conduits for that love and concern. I knew I could always invite myself around for a meal from time to time, or just turn up for a chat and a welcome change of scenery. I had a standing invitation for Christmas and New Year's Day, and I always accepted: first, because they were the closest thing I had to a family; second, because to be alone on those days is to feel the full force of isolation and not belonging. In future years I declined similar offers from other well-meaning and kind but less well-known people because I felt the odd one out. Being with such people simply deepened my sense of having no family; but I could truly relax with Mike, June and Maureen because we had a shared history, and I didn't in the least feel awkward. Because of this, I could be myself with them.

And when Maureen's son Peter visited, we were able to renew our friendship and share our enthusiasm for sport. Simply knowing that they were close by and always available made such a difference. I may have felt terribly lonely at times, but I knew deep down that they were there for me should I ever need them. Without them, it is unlikely that I would have made it through the winter of 1979.

The new year began, and I was still desperately short of money. My correspondence with John Honey contains occasional requests for money for books and examination fees which total over £200, but I felt too proud to reveal my true financial needs, so I struggled on in silence. On the other hand, there were some positives. One example is a letter dated February 1980 in which I mention my father: *Incidentally, I have heard from my father through an intermediary Swiss trust company and although nothing has yet materialised, I will keep you informed of developments.* John expressed his absolute delight to hear of this, particularly after his abortive attempts years earlier to contact my father.

However, this was of no direct help with the financial difficulties I was experiencing. I had moved downstairs to the smaller and cheaper front room to save money, but when in April the landlady increased the rent by 35 per cent and raised the utility rates substantially, I asked John for an increase to £35 per week, noting also that the average university student grant at that time was £41.50 per week. John's reply contained an assurance and a proposal. He would forward my request to the Trustees, but he also asked me to consider moving to the hostel he was preparing to open in nearby Spencer Avenue. I agreed to a temporary increase in my allowance to £35 per week, and that I would move to No.13 Spencer Avenue after completing my exams on 17th June, at which point I would pay rent to the Homes.

Spencer Avenue was yet another example of John Honey's amazing visionary thinking. At that time, children in care were largely left to fend for themselves once they reached the age of 18. What John recognised – and perhaps my difficulties helped him to make the case for this to the Trustees – was that those leaving care needed supportive transitional arrangements. My situation was particularly precarious since I lacked family support, financial means and secure accommodation. In addition, should I fail my exams yet again, the kind of accommodation and on-site support the Spencer Avenue project offered would be critical for my emotional and physical well-being.

I could describe my feelings on moving into No.13 in a variety of ways. It was like a breath of fresh air, a flood of light and a huge burden lifting from my shoulders. My main thought was that I no longer needed to worry about being evicted if I couldn't pay the rent. This was something that played on my mind quite literally every day during my time at Mayfield Road. By the time I moved into No.13 I had amassed a debt of about £300, equivalent to several weeks' allowance. I felt so ashamed about it that I hadn't mentioned it to anyone, fearing that it might destroy my relationship with John Honey and the Trustees. Now, I was still worried about how I was going to repay the bank, but at least I wasn't experiencing sleepless nights, stress headaches and unhelpful introspection fuelled by anxiety. In this way, No.13 provided an immensely helpful level of security and support that greatly improved my mental health.

I was eventually able to share my secret with 'Auntie' Winnie (Miles), a middle-aged single lady who was the warden of No.13. I told her that I would use my coming university grant to gradually repay the debt. She, however, with her greater wisdom and experience, saw that I would need every penny of my grant and, despite her own very limited means, decided to pay my debt in full. My pride initially resisted her generosity, but I could see that she was resolute, so I very reluctantly agreed. Because of my long history of being dependent on the generosity of others, I accepted her help with a sense of inadequacy and a degree of self-loathing, realising full well that I could not provide for myself. It felt humiliating even if the intent was to bless me. The coming months would show me just how fragile my financial affairs would remain and just how important Winnie's sacrifice was to my well-being.

Winnie blessed me in other ways too. I was able to talk over my hopes and fears with her in ways I had not been able to do with any other adult. It wasn't that Mike, June and Maureen weren't helpful or supportive, but I felt I was 'dumping' on them and that they would inevitably always see me as 'a Spurgeon's child' rather than the independent adult I aspired to be. Winnie was different. She had adult children of her own and had no past history with me, so to her I was a young man trying to make his way in the world rather than 'a Spurgeon's child'.

That was particularly important to me, because I was trying to shake off my in-care identity with all its negative associations. I still kept my Spurgeon's past a secret from my fellow students for fear that they would drop me or pity me. Even so, sometimes it proved impossible to conceal those things when conversations naturally turned to the subjects of home, parents and family. For example, I would attempt to impress girls from the college, but soon realised that if I was ever introduced to their parents, I would naturally be asked personal questions, and my answers would put an end to the relationship. As I have already said, what self-respecting parent would want their daughter forming a relationship with a young man with a long history of institutional care, no place to call home, no parents or family and no solid prospects?

So the girl thing wasn't worth even trying. But what weighed the most was that I was carrying so much emotional baggage that I couldn't even trust myself to make something of my life. On the rare instances when I trusted people with my secret, I would put a brave face on it. On one occasion one person responded, *I would never have guessed! You seem to have handled it okay.* I gave what I thought was a mature response, *Oh, you never get over these things completely. You simply learn to view them in their proper perspective.* It was a rationalisation that I was trying hard to believe was true. But it was a lie. I was in denial. Yes, I was containing my emotions to a point, but I knew I could not plug the 'emotional volcano' for ever. Apart from anything else, the pain, anger and fear of rejection I felt severely limited my relationships with my peers. I just could not completely relax and 'be myself', afraid that people would not like what they saw. And that of course simply fuelled my pain and self-loathing. It didn't help either that my acne seemed uncontrollable and further undermined my self-confidence.

None of these things, of course, bothered Winnie. What she saw was another young man trying earnestly, if somewhat falteringly, to make something of his life and to avoid the mistakes made by his mother and grandmother. In fact, having been through a painful divorce herself and successfully raised two children, she probably understood me more than most. Instead of quick or easy answers, she offered me something much more valuable – a listening ear and practical help. In so doing, she showed that she cared. She stayed with me through it all. That isn't to say that we didn't have our differences. But there was a level of mutual respect which meant we could be completely honest with each other.

So I experienced life at No.13 as an oasis of calm compared with Mayfield Road. For one thing, the rooms were larger, brighter and better decorated. And I didn't have to keep feeding the gas and electricity meters, worry about debt or about being fed, but most of all I was able to talk to Winnie instead of resorting to damaging internal dialogue.

But I still loved reading, and despite my lack of money still couldn't resist a bargain. Walking down Earlsdon High Street one afternoon in mid-1980, I came across a tattered cardboard box of remaindered books selling for a few pence and alighted on two in particular. One was called *So You're Lonely* by Roy Trevivian. He was a Christian, so I thought he might identify with my situation and have some answers for me. The other book was called *Mister God, This Is Anna* written by a man called Fynn: it appeared to be a true but tragic story about a girl who died at a very young age. Both books had a very positive and timely impact on me.

Trevivian's book was based on his experience of many years of mental illness and his work as a chaplain at the Mayflower Centre, a Christian community centre in Canning Town, which was at that time one of the most deprived parts of east London. I found myself underlining passages time and time again: 'Here is a man who understands how I feel,' I thought. But his main legacy was to give me (and I am certain many others) hope that Jesus understands and is always present to help. The book still occupies an honoured place on my bookshelf, and I still turn to it from time to time to treasure its timeless message of hope. A wonderful book!

Fynn's book is bittersweet. The central character is six-year-old Anna who lives in the East End of London and possesses amazing spiritual insight but who, at the age of seven, dies in an accident. Anna refers to God as 'Mister God'. I warmed to Anna's innocent simplicity and directness when talking about her friendship with Mister God. I especially liked her observation that the point of church meetings is to listen to the message and then go outside and put the message into practice. Her understanding of life with God was so clear and uncluttered compared with my experience of religion, which often seemed so complicated and impenetrable. Perhaps there was an alternative after all.

I had entered a period of welcome calm, but I was still anxious about my exam results. Again, my subject knowledge or intelligence was not at issue: it was rather my appalling exam technique. I just couldn't seem able to get my thoughts down on paper quickly enough within the allotted three hours! When in early August the results arrived, I was again thoroughly disappointed.

Once again, I had not done myself justice. I had taken four A-levels to increase my chances of getting to university. All the extra hard work and the grind of the previous two and a half years had resulted in a D and an E. The good news was that this would be sufficient for me to get a place on some kind of degree course. The bad news was that I would probably have to make do with a polytechnic rather than a university and with a degree course that was unpopular. My grades were ridiculously low, just one point above the absolute minimum required. Who on earth was going to want *me*? Well, within a couple of weeks I knew the answer: I received offers of an interview from both Teesside Polytechnic and Trent Polytechnic (Trent Poly). I decided to try Trent first, not least because it was located in the city of Nottingham, only an hour's journey from Coventry.

I really enjoyed my interview with Dr Christine Bellamy, the course tutor. With her jet-black, short, cropped hair and slim early 30s figure, she seemed to me too young to be a course tutor. Yet there was no mistaking her quick, sharp intellect and enquiring mind. She quickly put me at my ease, and we had a really good discussion about politics and current affairs. What I most appreciated was that she encouraged me to develop and justify my opinions rather than discounting them as unworthy of expression. I remember one of her statements: 'public opinion – whatever that is!' That has made me think about 'public opinion' and how it is formed ever since. At the end of the interview, Dr Bellamy put me out of my misery by offering me a place on the Bachelor of Arts Public Administration (BAPA) course. This was the public sector version of Business Studies and was designed to train undergraduates for careers in the public sector. It was a four-year course with the third year being a year-long vocational placement. I could now at long last apply for my university grant and think about the next few years. It was a huge burden off my shoulders!

Winnie was of course delighted for me, as were John, Maureen, Mike and June. But if I thought for one moment that I would no longer need their help, I was very much mistaken. But at the time I enjoyed the relief and excitement and set out to find student accommodation.

Chapter 16

Nottingham

Predictably, the best accommodation had already been snapped up by existing undergraduates and those who had been offered places well before me. I eventually alighted on a draughty old house three miles from the poly in the suburb of Carlton. I shared this with five other first-year male students and managed to secure the privacy of the only single bedroom in the house.

The rent was very expensive at £18 per week, but our landlady Mrs M stressed that this included breakfast. However, within a few weeks the 'breakfast' had become one egg per person per day. In addition, we were told not to use the central heating or else Mrs M would be forced to increase the rent to cover these costs. As we were later to learn, other students were paying £5 per week or less (exclusive of bills) for similar accommodation. So we were definitely being exploited and decided to find cheaper accommodation as soon as possible.

In the meantime, winter was setting in and it was impossible to keep warm in the house since Mrs M had also banned all electrical heating equipment. So one evening we hunted around for alternatives and found an old paraffin heater in the garden shed. Here was a cheap form of heating and so we lit it up. Within a few minutes we were enjoying our new-found source of heating in the main sitting room. We were feeling very pleased with ourselves until quite unexpectedly the heater erupted into flames. Our main concern was that the heater would explode. But after our initial shock and bewilderment passed we wound some string around it and gingerly dragged it out of the sitting room, through the kitchen and out into the garden, where it eventually burnt itself out.

But we now had another problem: the sitting room and the whole of the ground floor reeked of paraffin. Should Mrs M pay us one of her unannounced 'visits', she might immediately evict us. These visits were (according to her) to check that we were okay, but to us she was simply checking that we weren't using any form of heating that would eat into her profit. We thought we could disguise or smother the paraffin smell by spraying our deodorants around the ground floor. But no matter what we tried the paraffin smell persisted. We also realised that even if the deodorants did disguise the smell, we didn't have a convincing explanation for why we'd sprayed so much around that it made our eyes smart.

We were now starting to panic, but then I noticed one of the students cooking his supper in the kitchen and making a bad job of it. I suddenly realised that if we burnt some food then the smell would be strong enough to cover the paraffin and deodorant, thus providing a plausible cover story. As it happened, a few slices of bread toasted on the grill and wafted around the ground floor were sufficient to disguise our misdemeanour. An hour later, Mrs M appeared, and we were able to apologise for our poor culinary skills.

But we were stuck with a cold house and the threat of eviction for breaking the rules. I found the cold unbearable and decided to resurrect one of my Mayfield Road money-saving methods which was to use empty glass bottles with warm water and place them on my lap and under my feet. I didn't have enough money for a hot water bottle because my student grant was delayed and arrived several weeks late. In addition, an administrative error delayed payment of my Spurgeon's allowance for about two weeks, so I was really struggling to make ends meet. When my grant finally arrived I purchased a hairdryer which I used to take the edge off the cold in my room.

I moved out in mid-November to temporary lodgings and then in February 1981 I moved to a two-bedroom terraced house in the mining community of Bulwell, to the west of Nottingham. The main attraction of 10, Ockerby Street was that it was cheap at less than £4 per week. And no wonder: the landlord had spent very little money on it over the years. For example, the rear bathroom wall had a large, half-inch crack down the length of it which let the daylight in, and the main fuse had been replaced with a thick metal nail to prevent the electrics from shorting out (but creating a dangerous fire hazard)! But it was very cheap, and it was home. I stayed there for the next 18 months and thoroughly enjoyed the company of my housemates Andy, a geology postgraduate from Yorkshire, and Andy, an Accounting undergraduate from Leicestershire. Both had a great sense of humour and were fantastic company. None of us were particularly house proud and we happily shared the chores and the bills. Post-grad Andy was often away on field trips and the other Andy spent a lot of time studying at the poly. When we did all meet up, it would invariably be at the Golden Ball pub just a five-minute walk up the road.

Ockerby Street gave me the stability I needed during my first two years. This turned out to be critical in light of the very difficult issues I was facing at the time. For one thing, my finances remained precarious. Winnie had been right to caution me that my student grant wouldn't spell the end of my financial challenges, but nevertheless I was determined to be financially independent of Spurgeon's support. This was almost a badge of honour for me. After all, I was now 21 years old and had been reliant on Spurgeon's charity for almost 20 years. Could I really justify taking any more money from the Homes? Not that I wasn't grateful, but I strongly felt that I should by now be much more independent. I also knew that I didn't always spend my money wisely and so I felt that it would be wrong to ask for money to compensate for those poor choices.

During the previous November, John Honey had enquired as to my financial means, and I had told him about the administrative delays and my subsequent cash-flow problems. He was very sympathetic and agreed to review my needs in early 1981. That January I felt confident enough to tell him that, *from now on I will be able to cover myself [financially]*. I also mentioned that I was planning to leave Spencer Avenue as a vacation bolt-hole by Easter, because I would be making my own out-of-term accommodation arrangements. I signed off with heartfelt thanks for all the help Spurgeon's had given me over the past 18 years. It felt as if I was at long last cutting the umbilical cord with Spurgeon's.

But it was a false hope.

My continuing inability to effectively manage my financial affairs created major strains on my emotional health. One of my deepest fears was returning to the days of mounting debt, and this resulted in gnawing anxiety, sleeplessness and fear of the future.

I knew that John and the Trustees would never let me go under, but I had a very strong desire to finally be free and independent of help, even though trying to go it alone was a high-risk strategy because I was on my own with no relatives to support me and still carrying a heavy load of emotional baggage. I was also frequently fearful that I would not pass my second- and fourth-year exams. And I was also trying to work out what I believed about the world, the universe and everything. And why.

I had entered polytechnic as a Christian of sorts, but one who had been mauled by Andy M the committed Marxist, gently mocked by other freethinkers, and tolerated by my peers and lecturers alike. I could not hold my own intellectually, and although I felt unequal to the task of defending what I believed, I still had a deep-seated belief in the awe-inspiring Creator God I encountered at 'the hole in the wall' as a child. Because of this, I was delighted to get acquainted with members of the Christian Union (CU) midway through the first term of my first year.

What I most appreciated about the CU members was their commitment to their faith and their friendship. For the first time since leaving Spurgeon's three years earlier I had a peer group with which I felt comfortable. We shared each other's joys and sorrows as various individuals got married, experienced relationship difficulties and faced serious health issues. I learnt much from them and was able to identify myself with confidence as a Christian to my fellow undergraduates and lecturers. Little by little I was sorting out my beliefs and reasons for belief. But I still found it hard to critique the views presented to me during lectures and in the course text books. These were dominated by left-wing, left-of-centre and even Marxist perspectives, with a smattering of liberal and conservative authors such as Roger Scruton, Robert Nozick, Karl Popper and Hannah Arendt. As far as I could determine, my lecturers all shared these secular views and seemed to have no time for God. And although the course leader, Dr Bellamy, and my political theory lecturer, Mrs Whitebrook, encouraged us to think for ourselves, it was difficult as a new undergraduate to swim against the strong leftish tide in the absence of a mentor or lecturer with the intellectual ability to make an alternative case. As a result I tended to hold the two streams of thought in parallel. I would not allow my academic studies to threaten what I sensed was true; yet I was incapable of critiquing my academic studies which I knew to be fundamentally atheistic. This uneasy balancing act was not helped by my CU friends' inability to answer my faith-related questions regarding suffering, Christian factionalism and widespread injustice.

During the course of that year I read widely about Christianity and other philosophies and wrote down my thoughts on a number of topics which were immensely important to me, but not seemingly at all important to my

CU peers. For example, the issue of suffering was very real at that time because my mother had asked a mental health tribunal to release her from St Augustine's Hospital. I had been informed of the tribunal hearing but didn't feel I had anything to contribute, given the complex nature of her condition and my inability to care for her.

All of this meant that I became increasingly frustrated with my Christian peers and my own inability to develop a Christian critique of the prevailing secular ideas. So I was glad to discover a book which seemed to resonate with my sense of frustration. *Youthquake* was written by an Anglican clergyman called Kenneth Leech. I immediately identified with his anger at the Church's apparent indifference to social injustice: he was very good at pointing out such injustice and urging the Church to do more. However, he was weak on practical answers, and his Christian faith seemed to be based less on the centrality of Christ and historical Christian orthodoxy than on a mishmash of Marxist/Socialist doctrine with a Christian 'love thy neighbour' veneer. It seemed to me that he had done a good job raising issues but had failed to propose a robust and genuinely Christian response.

Unfortunately, this led me to conclude that Christianity was fundamentally flawed: at best, ineffective as an agent of social justice; at worst, legitimising the unjust status quo. What I failed to understand in my immaturity and righteous anger was that it was the Church that was flawed and not Jesus Christ, the foundation and cornerstone of its faith. I was throwing the baby (Christ) out with the bathwater (the Church). But I could not see that at the time and so jettisoned both my faith in Christ and the Church.

Perhaps it would be more accurate to say that I put my faith 'on hold' while I searched for the answers my Christian peers could not provide. I told my friends that until I found answers to what I considered to be fundamental questions, I would no longer call myself a Christian. I sensed their sadness.

By late February I was dating a lovely Turkish student called Ayşe (pronounced Eye-sheh). She was in her final year of a textiles design degree, and her expertise helped me to develop a well-overdue sense of fashion. As it happened, I also had the resources to buy more fashionable clothes: at about that time I received £3,500 from the insurance account my father had set up for me as part of his settlement with my mother. I had never had so much money before! I spent the bulk of it on Ayşe and myself. I remember buying lots of Italian clothes and shoes and going out to expensive restaurants. It felt good to be able to enjoy myself and to dress fashionably in ways that my peers admired and made me feel good about myself. However, there were two problems: I was not monitoring my expenditure and I was not applying myself to my studies. My days and nights were filled with having a good time with my lovely girlfriend.

The crunch came when I failed the June exams miserably. I would have to spend the summer revising for resits in early September. It was yet another academic failure, bringing back all the fears and unhelpful internal dialogue of previous failures. I found it hard to believe that I had put myself in this position yet again. This failure was compounded by another recurring issue: I was once again several hundred pounds in debt. I had not only spent my 'inheritance' but also some of the bank's money, and it was threatening legal action to recover the debt. It was my own fault. On top of this, Ayşe would be returning to Turkey in July to help manage her father's textile factory. She had agreed to do this in return for support for her training in textile design, so she had no choice but to return. She wanted me to follow her to Turkey once I had graduated, and we had several conversations about that. But once she returned to Turkey, I was able to look at things more objectively and realistically. I knew that I wouldn't cope with moving away from all I knew, with no real prospects, and having to learn a new language and adapt to a very different culture. And I also knew myself well enough that I couldn't wait for three more years to marry her. I was still only 21 years old – far too young to commit to massive changes that I didn't feel equipped to deal with. So in August, during a very tearful telephone conversation (on both sides), I told Ayşe that I wouldn't be coming to Turkey and wouldn't be marrying her. Even though I knew in my head that it was the right decision for *both* of us, I found it exceedingly difficult emotionally to utter the words that finally shattered her dreams. I hated myself for it. This had been my first serious relationship, and Ayşe had affirmed me in so many different ways. In particular, I was very grateful to her for helping me feel good about myself.

I was also grateful for John Honey's continued help. I phoned him in late July in a distraught state telling him about the large debt and my exam failures. He was so concerned that he immediately drove to Nottingham to speak face-to-face with me. As a result, he took care of the overdraft and offered me a room at Spencer Avenue to reduce my costs and provide a suitable environment to revise for my resits. It was somewhat humiliating to again need to accept financial assistance and to return to Spencer Avenue. I had thought I was able to stand on my own two feet, but it was clear that I still had some way to go. Nevertheless, I wasn't in a position to refuse, so I gratefully accepted John's help. My letter dated 23rd September 1981 describes the results of this help: *I am happy to report that I passed all of my exams thanks mainly to the month I spent in peace and quiet at Spencer Ave.*

John also asked the Trustees on my behalf for help with my cash-flow problems, given that my late exam results delayed my second-year grant by several weeks. He also provided the same assistance in the second term of that year. Without that I would have had great difficulty continuing my studies because, as the same letter stated: *I do not think my own bank manager is prepared to lend me money . . . [unless] it involves interest repayments.*

John's reply is typically gracious: *I am pleased that the Trustees have been able to help you during a sticky period, and I know that you will feel able to return to me at any other time I can be of assistance.*

And the first-year exam failure would not affect the final class of my degree because it was a qualifying year only; it was the second- and fourth-year exams that would be crucial. In this way I was able to make a new start, financially and academically. I also re-joined the Christian Union, putting my unanswered questions 'on hold' until I felt better able to handle them. I intended to enjoy the friendship of these and other undergraduates, to apply myself to my studies and to keep my finances on an even keel.

By the end of the second academic year my finances were in reasonable shape and, much to my surprise and the surprise of my peers, I came top of my year's exam results. Suddenly, I was very popular with my peers who were intrigued to know how I had managed to progress from bottom of the first year to top of the second year. In truth, the explanation is that I correctly predicted which exam questions would be asked and, free from financial and relationship worries, I was better able to concentrate on my studies. It was also significant that this was the first time *ever* during my education that I had *not* had to repeat the same exams in order to progress to the next stage of my education. It was quite a personal achievement.

I spent the summer of '82 at Spencer Avenue feeling very pleased with myself. In addition to my impressive exam results, I had also secured a well-paid and well-resourced 12-month work placement with Gloucestershire County Council's Personnel Department as a Personnel Trainee. So for the first time in a very long while I felt I was on the front foot and not just reacting to failure and disappointment.

I quickly found a room in a shared house not far from the Gloucestershire County Council Shire Hall. The four others in the house were single too and apart from minor niggles, the arrangement worked for all of us. When one of them left, my fellow undergraduate Denise, who had also secured a traineeship at the same place, moved in and we gradually got to know each other better.

Work for both of us consisted of placements within different sections of the Personnel Department: Health and Safety,

Workforce Planning, Management Services and Employee Relations.

Denise and I walked the mile or so to the Personnel offices in Lower Quay Street each day to continue our training. If truth be told, these placements weren't really 'work', but they did help me understand how the personnel department worked and prepared me for a longer period in employee relations: this introduced me to the world of industrial relations, including negotiations between the council and large public sector trades unions. I remember being particularly impressed by a certain Mr Bunce, one of the employee relations trainers, who seemed to have a near-perfect mastery of employment law and its practical applications. Whatever question was put to him and however obscure, he always seemed to have an answer. I was so impressed that I wondered if personnel management, as it was then termed, could be a possible career for me. After all, it was only a further year before I would need a job, and that seemed worryingly near.

As it was, such thoughts were increasingly eclipsed by my deepening friendship with Denise, and after several months we started dating. But by the time the work placement in Gloucester was drawing to an end I had concluded that I would need to end the relationship very gently. And I also knew that would not be easy.

From a work perspective the placement was a success and the salary kept me out of debt. But as I made my way back to Nottingham my main priorities were to do myself justice in the final exams and to find a way to end my relationship with Denise.

Chapter 17

Goodbye Academia

I started that year in good spirits. I had all to play for. I shared a ground-floor flat in the suburb of West Bridgford with a final-year quantity surveyor called John, and we got on very well. One major advantage of the location was that it was adjacent to the Trent Bridge cricket ground and close to Nottingham Forest and Notts County football grounds. During the winter we would hear the roar of the crowds as a goal was scored. In summer the cheers coming from the Trent Bridge crowd signified a wicket or a boundary.

Although I was determined to do myself justice academically, I became distracted by my new-found hobby: the late-night radio phone-in. I made my first call to the local radio station Radio Trent in response to a dare one night. It lasted only a few minutes but I was hooked. During that year (1983–84) I regularly phoned in to debate topics as varied as the national miners' strike (then in full swing), cohabiting, and tactical voting. But the show started at midnight and left me deprived of sleep and struggling to concentrate during lectures the following morning.

One advantage of the final year was that we were able to choose the subjects that we preferred. I dropped as many of the maths- and statistics-based subjects as possible but could not escape the dreaded compulsory economics module. My absolute favourite and my strongest subject was political theory. By now I was savvy enough to know which books to read to balance the left-leaning reading lists recommended by most but not all of the tutors. My favourite at the time was Professor Karl Popper. I had read his two-volume masterpiece *The Open Society and Its Enemies* the previous year and liked both his analysis of totalitarianism and his defence of liberal democracy. So, I was happy to take his critiques of public and political policymaking as the thesis for my fourth-year research project, and the good mark I received for that put me on course for a very good final grade. However, the downside was that I spent far too much time on the project at the expense of the other five subjects I was studying, which included my weakest subject: economics. For some reason this was something I simply could not master, and I feared it would drag down my final grade.

Eventually, the critical exam period commenced. I had been honing my revision technique and forcing myself to write a variety of answers to anticipated questions, so I knew I was as prepared as I could be. But it was still a tense time for all of us and I knew that I would struggle with the economics paper. And so it proved. What I did not foresee was that I would oversleep on the morning of my political theory exam, eventually arriving about 20 minutes late! I remember my tutor Mrs Whitebrook looking horrified and hurrying over to ask, 'What happened?!' My answer didn't make her feel any better.

The impact of my lateness was that I was awarded a 2:2 grade instead of the expected 2:1 by the narrowest margin possible. I was so disappointed with myself, fearing that this would affect my chances of getting a decent job. It also meant I could not pursue a planned Master's degree in personnel management at Sheffield Polytechnic. My academic career was at an abrupt end, and I now had no choice but to apply for jobs.

Feeling that I shouldn't set my sights too high, I applied for the post of Higher Clerical Officer with the Birmingham Health Authority. This proved to be good interview practice and I decided to aim a little higher and applied for a personnel trainee job with what I shall call Shiredown Council. I was shortlisted, interviewed and offered the job. But I wanted something more fulfilling than another trainee role so I declined and it was then offered to Denise who accepted it. I was hoping that we would find employment a good distance apart and that the relationship would gradually die a natural death so I wouldn't have to go through another Ayşe-like painful parting.

In early August I was offered an interview for a Senior Personnel Officer job in Cardiff. I spent the journey reading and re-reading the job description and rehearsed answers to possible questions. All the while the weather began to deteriorate, and by the time I reached Cardiff it was overcast and raining hard. As the train drew into the station I was suddenly overcome by a sense of dread: the city looked as grey as the leaden sky above. I began to think, 'This place looks so depressingly grey and dark: I don't think I could live here!' This just added to my interview nerves and the thought that perhaps I was aiming too high and was therefore bound to fail the interview. All of this led to another thought: why don't I just make my excuses and simply take the next train home? It took all my courage to face my fears, to put one deliberate step in front of the other and propel my body through the station exit into the city centre.

The interview came and went and I was told that if successful I would be invited to a second interview. A few days later I received a very nicely typed invitation to a second interview. I was elated. Clearly they thought I had what it took to do the job, and this was a huge confidence boost, dispelling any doubts that I had aimed too high. This time I would be facing three interviewers: Jenny, Clive and their boss and head of HR, Bob. It was Bob I would have to convince of my worth.

The second interview lasted a lot longer than I had expected and after almost two hours I was mentally and physically exhausted. I had given it everything I'd got. After several days of anxious waiting with no news, I concluded that I would not be offered the job and started looking for other vacancies. However, the following week I received another nicely typed letter asking me to phone Jenny. I was puzzled. But when I called from a public phone box, Jenny explained that she could not get me on my home number, and so she had written to me. She informed me that I hadn't got the job but had nonetheless performed very well at the interview. I couldn't bear to hear any more. It was as I had feared: I hadn't got the job. I interrupted her to say that I too didn't think I'd done well enough, thanked her, hung up and returned home feeling completely dejected. It was now late August and I really needed to find a job to make ends meet and get some structure and routine into my life. But as hard as I searched, I couldn't find anything.

Three days later I received another letter from Jenny asking me to call again. This time Jenny said, 'I wanted to tell you that the employee relations job has gone to someone with more experience, but we have decided to create a completely new post at the same grade and offer this to you. What do you think?' This was incredible! I was being offered a job that had been specially created for me, at a level that most new graduates could only dream of and with a starting salary almost twice that of my peers. Jenny explained to me what the job would involve but I wasn't able to take it in: I didn't ask any questions except to agree that I would start my first real job on 10th September 1984 with the grand sounding title of Senior Personnel Officer (Manpower and Special Projects). Wow!

Chapter 18

Hello Cardiff

Nottingham had been a good place to live – not too far from important means of support in Coventry, inexpensive and with plenty to entertain me – but I always knew that it was a temporary rather than permanent abode. I had happy memories and some painful ones too but, on the whole, I was sad to be leaving.

Part of my sadness came from having no place that I could truly call 'home'. Mike, June, Winnie and Maureen had always made me welcome whenever I visited, and, as I have said, I knew that they would always offer a bed for the night, a nourishing meal and a listening ear whenever I needed it. But unlike so many of my peers I was forced to live on the move. So often I felt like a tortoise carrying my home on my back. It was so burdensome, and the move to Cardiff illustrated this. My 'home' was all that I could physically carry. There was much I wanted to retain but had to dispose of because of this limitation. At that point my home consisted of a small portable black-and-white TV, two large hi-fi speakers and three hi-fi separates, plus whatever clothes I was wearing and any that I could pack into two large, light-brown PVC suitcases. I couldn't take many clothes because much of the space in the cases was taken up by the three hi-fi separates. I had bought the hi-fi units, speakers, TV and a stainless-steel Omega Speed Master watch with some of the money my dad had left me. As they were all I had left of my inheritance, they had real sentimental value, so I always carried them with me despite the considerable inconvenience.

My next 'home' was a single room in the Lansdowne Hospital about two miles west of the city centre. It was also just a two-minute walk from the staff canteen that provided copious quantities of food at very reasonable prices. I enjoyed staying at Lansdowne which was no longer functioning as a hospital but housed other new recruits. One of these was Ruth, a newly qualified occupational therapist who had also recently started work and was staying at Lansdowne for the same reasons. After getting to know each other socially she invited me to come to her church, Calvary Baptist (or simply Calvary), just a ten-minute walk away. I found it easy to accept her invitation because I was familiar with Baptist churches and the way they did things. For the first time in years I felt able to pursue my interest in religion once again because I had now graduated and obtained stable employment.

So, in November 1984 I accompanied Ruth to a Sunday morning service: I was pleasantly surprised that I really enjoyed the service. It was so different from my previous experience of Baptist churches. For one thing, there were lots of young people and families in attendance. In addition, the worship was contemporary, with a band playing electric and classical instruments and using electric amplification. Most of all, the Rev. Byron Jones preached in a way that spoke to me personally. I was later to learn that this was what was termed 'anointed' preaching, where there is an unmistakable sense that God is speaking through the preacher directly to a person's concerns and circumstances. I regularly felt as if Byron was speaking to me personally, and I often came away thinking, 'How could he know that!' On other occasions he would issue a challenge or seemingly look directly at me and I would think, 'He's right, I've got to do something about that!' There was nothing judgemental or condemning in the way he spoke, just rather what I came to recognise later as the gently insistent conviction of the Holy Spirit prompting me to draw closer to God. This experience of the reality of God greatly impressed me, and my thinking about Christianity began to change. Christianity was becoming less an abstract theory or philosophy of life as I saw more and more of the reality of God's presence amongst his people. There were still times when I felt that what some people were experiencing was emotional and psychological turmoil or excitement, having little if anything to do with God being present. But that still left cases where people were visibly impacted and changed in ways that were, in my view, best explained by a personal encounter with God. I started to attend Calvary regularly, getting to know several older adults who opened their homes to me and I also made friends with other young people of my age.

But I still wanted answers to my questions about God and religion in general before I could commit to any specific religion or philosophy of life. Even so, my first few weeks and months at Calvary convinced me that there was more to Christianity than I had yet experienced or been led to believe.

Meanwhile, I eventually rented a room with two other men in a small, terraced house close to the city centre in a district called Splott. The name was a contraction of South Plotlands and was inhabited mainly by working-class descendants of people who had been employed by the defunct steel mill and sprawling docks. My landlord was an amiable Brummie called Kevin who worked as a medical physics technician at the nearby Cardiff Royal Infirmary. The other tenant, Michael, worked as a scientist at the large Dow Corning chemical works in the town of Barry, west of Cardiff. They were both great fun.

My office was on the 14th floor of what was then the Pearl Assurance building overlooking Cardiff Castle, Sophia Gardens and the Cardiff Civic Centre. It was by far the tallest building in Cardiff, and I would often sprint up the 14 floors on foot to test my level of fitness. The first week at work involved getting to know my colleagues and making contacts within the Authority and I bought myself a smart light-grey pinstriped suit to look the part.

I quickly realised that there was a lot to learn in a very short time. I had three main responsibilities: first, to provide employee relations to specific non-hospital-based services such as the huge laundry; second, to take a lead on the implementation of a new computerised workforce information system; and third, to do the detailed research and preparatory work for the implementation of competitive tendering for ancillary services such as cleaning and catering. But as the weeks and months went by I began to understand the magnitude of my responsibilities and it finally dawned on me that although my superiors thought I was capable, what they really wanted was someone who would simply get on with what was a very tough agenda without bothering them too much. But my duties demanded that I climb an incredibly steep learning curve and I don't think they realised that I was struggling to keep up with the demands of the job. These work pressures caused me a great deal of stress to the point that I began to experience blinding migraines for the first time in my life. I had accepted the job on the basis of a salary which was much higher than that of my peers, but I was now learning the hard way that the demands of the job were considerable – and perhaps beyond me.

On top of this my relationship with Denise was drawing to an end. I was fond of her but during this time I was gradually working out what was important to me in life, and it eventually became clear to both of us that we simply didn't want the same things, and so during the course of yet another unwelcome tearful phone conversation we agreed to remain friends but to go our separate ways.

Chapter 19

The Meaning of Life?

We all have a working philosophy of life, even if we can't explicitly state what it is. Denise's philosophy, it seemed to me, was: 'be a good person, live and let live, and have a good time'. I can see the merits of that philosophy but that wasn't enough to satisfy me. Was that *really* all that life and living was about? This question really mattered to me, so I didn't want to cop out and put off answering this question as if it wasn't important. But on the other hand, I wasn't about to uncritically swallow everything that religious adherents, including Christians, so earnestly professed.

So I decided to make a serious effort to answer the fundamental questions that kept bothering me. I had never really engaged with them effectively and reached a clear conclusion up to this point. But I was now willing and able to give them the detailed attention they deserved, and I knew that the task would require intense effort and as much open-minded honesty as I could muster. I also realised that I might even have to change some of my long-held cherished beliefs and ways of doing things.

Even from my earliest days, there were a whole host of questions I would ask from time to time. I soon realised that to make the task manageable I would need to identify a few key questions and would need some reference materials to help me work through them. In this I was helped enormously by Colin Chapman's *The Case for Christianity* which had been published just four years earlier. This book helped me clarify which questions mattered the most and brought me to the point of being willing to critically examine and evaluate the answers that Christians gave. Chapman examined how people of other faiths, such as Buddhists, Muslims and Jews, agnostics and atheists would answer these same questions. I ended up with ten basic questions which seemed to have been with me forever, even though I couldn't always put them into words. These were:

1. The Individual: Who or what am I?

2. The Meaning of Life: What's the point of it all?

3. Values: How are we to make moral choices?

4. Truth: Is it possible to know the truth about ourselves and the universe?

5. Love: What is love, and where can it be found?

6. Suffering: Why is there suffering, and how can we live with it?

7. Death: How do I face death? Is there life after death?

8. The Future of Man: What hope is there for the human race?

9. The Supernatural: Is there anything more than the physical world?

10. Evil: Is there any hope in fighting evil and injustice?[2]

At that time, questions seven and eight were the least pressing for me personally, with questions two, three and six the most important. This was because I was still wrestling with my own experiences of suffering and trying at the same time to make sense of tragic stories I would hear about from time to time in the news media. Question three was one of the first I remember asking myself as a child, and question two was important because the answer would help me make choices about my career and personal life, including who to marry. Of course, all ten questions are interrelated, and the answers overlap. But at that time the most pressing questions were to do with right and wrong, and purpose and suffering.

What I really appreciated about Chapman's approach was his willingness to hold the Christian worldview up to critical scrutiny, allowing non-Christians to provide their answers and inviting seekers like me to consider alternatives we might find more convincing. It seemed to me that in taking this approach he was taking quite a risk. But he clearly felt that the reader should, nonetheless, be invited to examine the evidence and to decide for themselves. This approach appealed to me, and I felt it showed a deep respect for me as an earnest seeker.

I found this journey of exploration incredibly stimulating. I was introduced to a broad range of ideas, some familiar to me and others completely new. There were the perspectives of psychoanalysts, Marxists, sociologists, existentialists, novelists, scientists, playwrights and humanists: each was allowed to speak for themselves in extensive quotes from their own works. This enabled me to weigh their responses to the ten questions in my own way and in my own time.

By Easter 1985 I had concluded that the Christian answers to those questions were more persuasive and more closely fitted the evidence than the alternative viewpoints. However, I found to my frustration that the answers seemed to generate even more questions. It seemed that each answer only moved the desired end further away. 'If only I could get an answer to the next question, I would be able to trust God for the rest of what I don't know!' It was all becoming rather self-defeating. Kierkegaard and Pascal helped me at this point. In Kierkegaard's view, human beings will never find *all* the answers they seek and be able to completely close the knowledge 'gap'. Our knowledge will always be limited, and I realised that I had to take a 'leap of faith' to bridge the gap. I felt rather reluctant: this was new and unchartered territory for me. But Pascal's 'wager' nudged me forward. Pascal suggested that we take that leap of faith and then explore where it leads. If it leads to God, all well and good: we will have gained something. If it does not lead to God, then we may well feel embarrassed but would have lost nothing. Christianity, I concluded, could not be proved conclusively by reason, but neither could it be disproved. It seemed at times that God was saying to me, 'Just trust me for what you *don't know* on the basis of what you *do know* about me!'

In this I was later helped by reading the works of Saint Anselm, in which he encouraged the same approach of 'faith seeking understanding'. He meant by this that we do not understand in order to believe, but rather believe (by faith) in order to understand. In this way, Anselm acknowledged the limits of our capacity to know everything and concluded that 'knowledge' could be revealed from the perspective of faith. In looking back, not long after my decision to 'leap', I realised that this is the way God has arranged things. There will always be a faith gap of some sort to which his response is, 'Just trust me!'

A couple of years later in 1987 I had a vivid dream that helped me understand this principle of faith in a very memorable way. In the dream, I was in a garden standing outside a well-used greenhouse in which there were plants and flowers. I was peering in and could see a lot from the outside, including what kind of flowers and plants there were, their colours, the shape of their leaves, which ones were in bud and which ones were in flower. But when I entered the greenhouse, my experience became much richer. From the inside I experienced things that I could not experience from simply looking in from the outside. For example, the air in the greenhouse was humid, warm and scented with the smell of plants and the soil. I could touch individual flowers, and because I was that much closer, I could see their leaves and flowers in greater detail. I could also see that some plants that seemed to be doing well from the outside were in fact, on closer inspection, doing poorly, and vice versa. So, although I could see and experience a great deal from the outside, my experience was incomplete and sometimes misleading. From the inside, my experience was qualitatively superior and my understanding of the plants and their environment more complete and more accurate. My different senses were also more fully engaged. What I'd done in entering the greenhouse was to cross the 'threshold of faith', and in so doing, I experienced reality in ways that were more complete and much more satisfying. And the more I got to know the 'Head Gardener' the more he revealed to me and the more my confidence in him grew.

So, by Easter 1985 I had intellectually assented to Christianity on the basis that it seemed to provide the best fit with my experience of the world and the best answers to the questions that were important to me.

But I now needed to discover God's plan for my life. This was one of the most pressing questions that I had identified as I read Colin Chapman's book. The importance of this issue had already been reinforced by a Campus Crusade for Christ conference in Birmingham in January 1985, and it is clear from my diary entries for the next year or so that this was my main focus and also my greatest struggle.

I threw myself into church outreach activities which enabled me to get to know members of the church very well, and I began to question whether my current job and career aspirations were in line with what God wanted for my life. I hadn't yet made the necessary effort to find out. But it is clear from my diary entries in August 1985 that I was thankful to God for bringing me to a new place of faith and that I was committed to serving him.

My need to resolve this issue was brought home to me very forcefully and unexpectedly about this time. My boss had been promoted and was therefore moving elsewhere from his sprawling 14th-floor office. That vacant office was coveted for several reasons, among them its panoramic views of the city. Although it was completely unrealistic to expect that I would ever be allowed to occupy it, I decided one blazing summer afternoon to wander in, take in the view and marvel at its spaciousness. It was the very same office in which I had been interviewed just a year earlier. I remember surveying both the panorama of Cardiff and the details of the office in awed silence and thinking to myself, 'I've made it! If I just get on with my job, then promotions will come and in 40 years' time I will be able to retire with a decent pension. By that time I will have found someone to marry, had children, bought a house and achieved the material and emotional security I have always strived for!' But that thought was unexpectedly followed by another thought, as if from nowhere: 'But is that what God wants you to do with your life?' My immediate response whispered under my breath was a very dejected, 'Oh no!' Even though I did not know at that time what God wanted for me, I suspected that it probably wasn't this. I felt very unsettled, but I also knew it was such an important issue that I had to face it honestly, with an open mind and an open heart. I expected it to be a struggle, and in this I wasn't wrong: the quest was to expose all my deepest fears and insecurities.

Chapter 20

So Much More ...

During this period of grappling with God's will for me, I found myself returning to Bonhoeffer's *The Cost of Discipleship.* My diary entries for October include my responses to Bonhoeffer's words on the hiddenness of prayer: I wrote out in full his four 'Stations on the Way to Freedom', which he wrote as he faced the prospect of execution by the Nazis. The four 'Stations' are self-discipline, action, suffering and death. In retrospect this seems rather 'heavy' for a young Christian trying to find his way in life, but it is a genuine reflection of my earnest desire to learn from those who had gone before me, even those who had paid the ultimate price.

In November I made a public declaration of faith and underwent adult baptism at Calvary. It was a bittersweet occasion: unlike the other baptismal candidate I had no family members or long-standing friends to support me. This was partly my own fault for not realising that I could and should invite some friends. And although my new-found Calvary friends did their best to support me on this important occasion, I did feel the absence of those who had known me longest.

This time of intense searching also explains why I felt the need to spend Christmas at an Anglican community of sisters based at Malvern Link, called the Community of the Holy Name (COHN). I had benefitted from a retreat there earlier in the year and enjoyed being in a setting that was peaceful, friendly and calming. I can't remember how I discovered the sisters, but I do remember that I did not want to repeat the previous Christmas when I ended up alone at Hamilton Street, having misled Kevin and Michael into believing that I was spending Christmas with family and friends. That time passed very slowly, with me watching the television, trying not to be envious of all the fun that other people were having and slowly drinking myself into a semi-inebriated state to dull the pain of loneliness. It wouldn't have been so bad if I hadn't made myself a massive lamb curry that I thought would feed me over the Christmas period but which gave me violent diarrhoea. I spent most of Boxing Day curled up on my bed in excruciating pain.

So a stay with the COHN sisters provided a very welcome alternative and it also meant that I could continue to explore God's purpose for my life. I should point out that several Calvary friends had invited me to join their Christmas family activities, but I knew from previous experience that I would feel very much the odd one out if I accepted such an invitation. For me, it was much better to be in an anonymous setting where I could be one of a crowd. I noted that the dozen or so others who came to the COHN at Christmas came for reasons similar to mine. I got to know Sister Pippa who was responsible for looking after guests, and we often had conversations about spiritual matters such as guidance and vocation. We didn't always agree but I really liked her sense of fun as well as her spiritual depth and maturity. I was also struck by the fact that she was very different from what I expected in a sister. She seemed to be very well educated, well informed about the world around her, well-travelled and happy in her chosen vocation. It really was possible to be intelligent, happy and holy at the same time! For me, she was a very gentle and caring benevolent 'big sister'. Most of all I'm sure that Pippa and the other sisters prayed that God would reveal his love and his purposes to each of us who found our way to their home.

A few days later, I travelled the short distance to Birmingham to attend the 'Acts 86' conference which was hosted by Michael Green, a Church of England clergyman whose name was familiar to me through his writings. He had invited John Wimber, an American pastor to minister to UK Christians. I had read several of Green's books over the years and found them immensely helpful in making the case for Christianity. However, this conference was about the specific area of 'signs and wonders', and it offered me a new way of thinking about and 'doing' Christianity. I attended the conference for two reasons. The first was that people at Calvary had clearly been impacted by John Wimber's ministry; the second was that although I had intellectually assented to Christianity and had been baptised, I sensed there was so much more to be discovered.

At that time I remember feeling 'stuck' and in need of a breakthrough. I realised that Christianity was a 'revealed' religion, and by giving intellectual assent to it I could look forward to an unveiling of that revelation from the standpoint of faith. But Christianity also claimed to be a supernatural religion, involving the believer in a spiritual encounter with a personal God. That sounded rather daunting and even scary to me, but because of my positive 'Hole in the Wall' experience as a pre-schooler I was expectant despite my nervousness.

As it happened, Calvary was, along with many other UK churches, entering a period of spiritual revival known as the 'charismatic renewal'. Christians were being encouraged not just to know *about* God but to know God in a personal way. In my particular case, I had a great deal of religious 'baggage' that would have to be dumped if I was ever to move from mere intellectual assent to a genuine experience of God's love and grace. Although I didn't recognise it at the time, a lot of this baggage was due to what Christians call 'legalism'.

Despite all the Christian input I had received over the years, I had largely failed to understand God's grace towards me: this could loosely be translated as 'God's unmerited favour', and it is absolutely central to Christian belief and experience. Legalism, on the other hand, is the complete opposite of grace: it is our human attempts to earn God's acceptance by what we *do*. And that was where I was at this time: I was fixated on pleasing God in order to gain his approval. The problem was that I regularly failed to do that. Consequently, I lived with a constant sense of guilt and self-condemnation, and although I would come to God for forgiveness and restoration, I knew I would inevitably fail again. It wasn't much fun feeling like a constant failure, trying desperately to meet God's standards in order to be acceptable to him. But I believed this was what God required of me and that there was no alternative.

I believe that my upbringing in care contributed to this way of thinking. Spurgeon's was run on rules which had some clear practical benefits: they ensured that expectations were clear to all and applied equally to everyone. Because of these rules, we all learned very quickly what was allowed and what was not. In this way, our behaviour was shaped by the rules. Going against the rules was routinely punished, and this tended to deter further infringements because of the very real threat of corporal punishment for major breaches. Lesser infringements incurred the loss of meals and privileges and the addition of multiple chores. What this communicated to me was: 'Follow the rules and you will be rewarded; disobey the rules and you will be punished.' I can see why such sanctions were necessary in order to maintain discipline and order, and I'm sure the Spurgeon's staff would have been mortified if they had known this was to prove an obstacle to my Christian development. But I think that being exposed to this environment for so many of my formative years meant that I had naturally incorporated this way of thinking into how I thought about God. This didn't become clear to me until I was asked to lead the Calvary youth group and attend a home group and found that some of the things I said were met with concerned looks. Slowly and very gently older Christians started to point me in the right direction, but although I understood the concept of grace in my head, it took much longer to affect my emotions and my behaviour. The rules-based mentality was so deeply ingrained that it would take more than a change in my thinking to remedy it: it would require a minor miracle. The charismatic renewal would begin that miracle.

Chapter 21

A New Direction

The term 'renewal' referred specifically to personal and corporate spiritual revitalisation, and, as I have mentioned, it was characterised by what were called 'signs and wonders'. This was a term derived from the New Testament and especially the Gospels and the Acts of the Apostles and refers to divinely empowered acts such as healing and exorcism that accompanied the proclamation of the gospel. The renewal also emphasised the need for spiritual growth and the exercise of spiritual gifts such as prophecy, praying in tongues and words of knowledge.

While most Christians at the time were aware of such things from their reading of the New Testament, John Wimber and his team had a track record of actually performing such signs and wonders. This was radically new, and John Wimber referred to it as 'doing the stuff'. His hypothesis was that Western Christians had unwittingly embraced a secularised and materialistic worldview that automatically ruled out present-day supernatural divine acts. As a result, most Christians didn't believe that God was either willing or able to act in these ways, and therefore lived a very truncated and cosmetic form of Christianity, focusing primarily on moral behaviour and an intellectual assent to

God's existence and his plan of salvation as described in the Old and New Testaments.

An early hint of what to expect had come some months earlier during a service at Calvary when I turned to greet a retired couple seated behind me called Fred and Edna. To my surprise they had tears running down their cheeks, so I asked them what the matter was, and Fred replied through the tears in a voice trembling with emotion, 'David, we've been such fools. We've been attending church for many years, and we thought that that was all there was to it. But now we know differently.' The difference was the tangible presence of God himself.

But this new approach was undoubtedly controversial, and while some endorsed Wimber's theology and practice, others were much more sceptical and critical. I was both undecided and intrigued. So when the opportunity came to attend the Acts 86 Signs and Wonders conference at the beginning of 1986, I unhesitatingly signed up. I was reassured that the conference was being led by Michael Green, who could be trusted to ensure that Wimber and his team were not promoting false teaching or suspect practices.

I therefore arrived at the conference with high expectations but determined to be first and foremost an observer and learner. What impressed me most was the complete absence of hype and Wimber's relaxed matter-of-fact approach. The teaching sessions were followed by 'clinics', sessions during which the teaching was applied in the form of healing prayer, exorcism, prophecy, etc. Individuals were then invited to publicly share what God had done for them during these clinics.

I left wanting to know more and was able to borrow some teaching tapes from other Calvary members. Like Fred and Edna before me, I was to learn that there was more to Christianity than I thought. At the very heart of Christianity is a living and active God who desires that his people 'do the stuff'. Most of the Calvary leadership were willing to provide opportunities to do just that.

So there were two ways in which my faith was gradually starting to develop: intellectual understanding, and the Spirit-inspired application of that faith. It was a steep learning curve, but I felt I was making progress. I was also making good friends at Calvary including a number of older adults: Gary, an American pastor, and his wife Trish; Colin and Lynette; and Dennis and Jane. These good people were instrumental in making me feel included and they all encouraged me in many ways.

But things were not going well at work. On 18th January, I wrote:

> The last two days have been hectic at work. The manpower figures haven't been crosschecking again and there was a last-minute panic. The new Personnel Department structure has a Scale 9 manpower planning post – I'm not sure whether I've got sufficient expertise or Authority-wide credibility to stand a chance of getting it, and I'm not sure God wants me to have it either. Still it's early days yet!

The Scale 9 post was one grade senior to mine, and I realised that I would probably have to compete for it. So there was a real possibility that I would be out of a job or at least transferred to another post by the end of the year.

In the meantime, I was still trying to discern God's purpose for my life. That Easter that purpose became clearer.

In April 1986 I found myself amongst other Calvary folk attending the week-long Spring Harvest Christian conference at Minehead in Somerset. This was the first time I had attended, and I really appreciated feeling part of something much larger than the local church. I particularly enjoyed the variety and quality of the teaching and the seminars on how to develop and use spiritual gifts. I found myself taking in as much as I could because so much of it was completely new to me. The calibre of the keynote speakers was impressive and included a man called Roger Forster who didn't seem to be ordained but led a large and growing church in south-east London. This was my first real introduction to what was known as the house church movement with its unashamedly charismatic emphasis.

There was another reason why I enjoyed the week so much: I made the acquaintance of yet another Christian young lady I shall call Christina. This was not at all intentional on my part, although it was probably inevitable that someone would catch my eye sooner or later. I can't remember much more about the conference itself, but my diary entry late on 27th April shows that I had reached some important conclusions and decisions, thanks both to the conference and my acquaintance with Christina: *For the last nine months I've been earnestly seeking God's will for me. I know that my heart isn't in NHS personnel management, my heart is in doing God's will, not my own.*

As part of my seeking God's will, I had been on three monthly retreats, but I still felt I was striving in my own power, *like Peter walking on the water and sinking.* The most significant part of that particular diary entry notes: *At Spring Harvest I committed my life to full-time Christian work.*

My diary also states that I had written to the then London Bible College (LBC, now the London School of Theology) and All Nations Christian College (All Nations) to ask about the availability of places for September 1986. I remember Christina strongly recommending LBC which she had attended before starting work as a church worker in a deprived neighbourhood in the East End of London. However, I wanted to give God ample scope to direct me, and as my Calvary friends Colin and Lynette had warmly recommended All Nations, I decided to apply there as well. What appealed to me was that All Nations was more hands-on than LBC and had a strong cross-cultural emphasis. I decided against applying for more than two Bible colleges: I wanted this to be an act of faith and so restricted my applications so that God could easily close down both options. So this was the 'fleece' I put before God, rather like Gideon in the book of Judges.

It wouldn't be the first time I had wrongly tried to force an issue, and my diary entry shows that I'm conscious of this. I note that a previous friendship with another young lady had withered because I was simply using it to overcome my fear of loneliness by trying to shape God's will to meet that need rather than seeking his will first and foremost:

> *With my background and just the way that my body at the age of 26 ½ years works my greatest need is to rid myself of the fear of being lonely . . . the cause*

of my disobedience. By taking away that distraction I am now free . . . I can now focus on his will – I have now no distractions.

I then wrote down some verses from Psalm 37 to remind myself of one of God's promises:

*Delight yourself in the L*ORD *and he will give you the desires of your heart. Commit your way to the L*ORD*; trust in him and he will do this: He will make your righteousness shine like the dawn, the justice of your cause like the noonday sun. Be still before the L*ORD *and wait patiently for him.*

I confess that simply writing that down didn't make it any easier in practice to *wait patiently*!

I shared all of this with Byron, adding that I felt a specific call to Muslims. His response was that Calvary would need to confirm that my sense of leading was correct. In early May I was elected to be a deacon for missions, which to my mind seemed to confirm just that. My diary entries for May and June record that I am *raring to go* with local evangelism and outreach, but also that I have resisted the temptation to skimp on revision for my professional personnel management exams: after all, those professional qualifications might prove useful in the future. It was also looking increasingly likely that I was going to be made redundant and would find it hard to find another job in Cardiff, so I would probably have to bid farewell to Calvary. So even having passed my professional exams I didn't feel relieved: I was facing redundancy and the real prospect of moving away from Calvary and having to find the money to finance Bible college. So I kept reminding myself of God's love for me in the face of *job doubts, no firm home or family or a clear future.*

I was falling in love with Christina and she introduced me to her co-workers in east London. The team was led by David and Jean. David was an ordained Church of England clergyman and Jean was a deaconess, but the whole team helped lead the estate-based congregation. What struck me about them was their joyful resilience and real concern for the people they served. They were assisted by Sue and Olaf who, like David and Jean, had two children. These fine Christians were the leaders of the ministry and the main focus of their work was among poor, working-class tenants living on a huge council estate, in very challenging conditions. Many of these people were unemployed immigrants struggling with personal issues.

I greatly respected what they were doing and realised that if Christina and I were to get better acquainted then I would need to move to London. I also realised that even should I receive an offer from LBC or All Nations, if Byron or Calvary decided that I should wait until the following year, then this would *probably spell the end of my relationship with Christina not least because we would both be almost 30 years old by the time I graduated and I'm not sure if either of us is prepared to wait that long.* There was also the major issue of finding the means to pay for the Bible school training. I thought Spurgeon's might help, but there was no guarantee, and it was unlikely that I could count on Calvary. I therefore decided to fast for a week to get a sense of the Lord's will, and once again entered some verses from Psalm 37 into my diary: *Commit your way . . . Wait patiently for him.*

In early August I was interviewed at LBC and was given a basic Bible-knowledge test. My embarrassingly poor results meant that I would be entered for the diploma and not the degree course. That wasn't what I wanted. The invitation from All Nations arrived during the last week of August and having arrived late for my interview I found the main college buildings closed for the summer vacation. I was beginning to wonder if my interviewers had forgotten about me when I heard a loud 'Helloooo!' behind me. I turned, and there was a middle-aged man with wavy black hair and a wiry frame sporting a multicoloured Peruvian-type jumper, arms aloft in a welcoming pose and with a big smile on his face. This was quite a contrast to the formal attire and manner of the LBC staff. I was later to learn that this was Martin Goldsmith, someone very well-known and highly regarded in UK Christian circles. But I didn't know that at the time. He was very likely unaware of just what a positive impact his greeting had on me, and how that put me very much at ease. He then led me through to the room where I was interviewed by him and two other colleagues. I loved it! The only question was, did they love *me* enough to offer me a place assuming there was a place available with just three weeks to go before the start of the new academic year? I knew that All Nations was an immensely popular and well-regarded college. Thankfully the answer came quickly, and I prepared to start my training in the second week of September.

By this time, I had concluded that I could contribute £1000 to the £3500 a year tuition fees. Spurgeon's agreed to contribute a further £2000, and extraordinarily generous friends at Calvary provided the rest.

I was both very relieved and highly elated. It was, humanly speaking, a miracle! As I looked back on the sequence of events since graduating, I could not but be impressed by the improbability of it all. This is how it all came about:

- I had been able to give my Shiredown job offer to Denise to weaken the relationship with her;
- I got the Cardiff job against the odds;
- Ruth and I lived in the same temporary accommodation for just a few weeks;
- Ruth invited me to Calvary;
- COHN offered me regular space to discern God's will for my life;
- Byron was my pastor at Calvary, a man with an anointed ministry;
- I found just the right book by Colin Chapman to help me work through my many questions;
- Calvary was going through renewal and growth at just the right time;
- John Wimber was at the conference where I could learn about charismatic Christianity;
- I was faced with virtually certain redundancy from my job and no obvious alternative employment;
- Spring Harvest provided me with the opportunity to make a commitment to full-time work;
- I met Christina at Spring Harvest who encouraged me to think about full-time Christian work and Bible college training;

- I received immediate confirmation of God's will by being elected a missions deacon;

- Colin and Lynette recommended All Nations to me;

- All Nations offered me a place very late in the academic year;

- I received provision of the finances for the All Nations training at very short notice.

All of these things were completely or largely beyond my control, yet they came together at just the right time. I am not a statistician, but I suspect that the probability of all of this happening in this particular way is exceptionally low indeed. For me, it was God's response to my trust in him.

Chapter 22

All Nations

The All Nations College motto is, aptly enough, 'From All Nations, to all nations' and it continues to have a fine reputation for training Christians for cross-cultural service. The campus is situated about 20 miles north of London on the Easneye estate. I was one of about 180 students comprising singles and married couples. About a third of these were non-British and came from about 30 different countries.

I felt very relaxed in my new surroundings because I had certainty for the next two years. I knew what I would be doing and, very importantly, where my 'home' would be. But it was also because the rules and routines, the chores, the large site, communal events and activities and the beautiful setting resonated deeply with my Spurgeon's years, and I slipped into the run of things with great ease.

I soon began to make friends, particularly among the other single men. Chief among these were Phil, Steve, Chris and Keith. I also formed good relationships with married couples such as Kerr and Karen and with staff members such as Vera, Tom, Walter and Ron. This was one of the outstanding strengths of All Nations: the staff were as much our friends as our teachers, and all of them accepted sacrificial salaries and simple lifestyles in order to keep our tuition fees at an affordable level.

All had a heart for cross-cultural mission and a desire to see us learn as much as possible.

This meant so much more than theological and theoretical learning, although I was soon to learn (yet again) just how embarrassingly little I understood my faith. No, the greatest learning for all of us was the business of getting on with and understanding people who were culturally, temperamentally and theologically very different from us. We learnt this mainly by living together and sharing ministry in local churches. In addition, we participated in memorable UK versus The Rest of the World team competitions including relay races around the estate and fiercely competitive football matches which in my case left a permanent physical mark!

There were also some very sophisticated pranks involving the kidnapping of my tutor Vera and the playing of Bach's Fugue and Toccata at a very loud volume during the small hours in the women's hostel. So college life was far from being 'all work and no play'. But there was still substantial work to be done, especially since I was taking the Cambridge Diploma in Religious Studies (CDRS) which required more work than the standard college syllabus. I had chosen the CDRS partly to improve my theological knowledge and partly with an eye to further theological study at another college or university. I was encouraged in that direction by Christina. We had begun dating just before I started at All Nations, and I could see she had high hopes for our relationship. I therefore began to see a lot more of her and travelled regularly to London.

On one particularly memorable evening we decided to go to a cinema in central London via the nearby Bow Road underground station. We managed to find two seats in the crowded waiting room and chatted while we waited for the train which was unexpectedly delayed. A while later we became aware of a commotion nearby caused by one particular man shouting and forcing his way through to the waiting room. He used his bare forearm to force open the heavy metal-framed door and gashed himself in the process, but without flinching. The people around us exited hastily within seconds and he sat opposite us. By then only Christina and I remained. I don't know why we stayed except that for some reason I didn't want to be intimidated into leaving. But I was praying silently and fervently for God's protection over both of us and for wisdom to know what to say and do (or not) while we waited.

The man was in his mid to late 30s, well built with dishevelled brown hair and a full beard. He wore a long dark-grey coat and robust brown shoes. He was menacing and muttering under his breath but with his eyes firmly focused on the floor. We said nothing, avoided eye contact and continued to pray while trying to appear calm. Quite unexpectedly and while still staring at the floor he suddenly asked us in a gruff voice, 'Are you Christians then?' We both answered together, 'Yes, we are.' After a few moments of silence he continued, 'What do you believe then?' To me it sounded more like a challenge than an enquiry. 'We believe in Jesus Christ. What do you believe in?' He grunted dismissively and after a few moments the train finally arrived: we got up and briskly walked out of the waiting room and onto the train. The whole encounter was very curious. It seemed like we were being challenged by a malevolent spiritual entity. The attempt to intimidate us failed, although in retrospect perhaps part of the plan was to get us on our own. Whatever the reason, the encounter was confrontational and challenging for both of us. The whole thing invited the question: 'How did he know we were Christians?' We were wearing normal casual clothes for an evening out and there was nothing to distinguish us from the others in the waiting room. Yet, his question was clearly designed to get us to confirm what he already seemed to know or suspect. The answer came later and from an unexpected source at All Nations.

In the meantime, I got to know Christina's co-workers better. They had chosen to work among some of the neediest people and in one of the poorest areas of London that regularly appeared at the bottom of national league tables of social and economic deprivation. The challenges they faced often demanded great courage, patience and wisdom. Both couples could have chosen much more congenial ministry settings.

I experienced first-hand one such challenge while staying with Olaf and Sue. One evening the front doorbell rang loudly and insistently. A young Asian-looking woman (who we shall call Ida) stepped hurriedly into the entrance hall carrying a baby in one arm and clasping the hand of a small primary aged boy (who we shall call Jim) with the other hand. Her face was etched with desperate terror. She was clearly very frightened by something or someone.

She and her husband Tom lived in a flat on the nearby high-rise estate, and Tom had become very angry with Jim, threatening him with serious harm. Ida had physically interposed herself between the two, and Tom had temporarily calmed down. But Ida knew that Tom was volatile and decided it was best to leave. She had attended the church Sunday services and knew that Sue and Olaf would protect her and the children. Olaf and Sue calmed her and led her and the children upstairs. Ida continued to worry that Tom would guess where she had gone and might very well follow her. We waited and prayed.

A little while later he did indeed turn up. Ringing the doorbell aggressively, he demanded to be let in. Olaf refused to open the door until he calmed down. But Tom became even angrier, threatening to kick the door down and take Ida and the children with him. He claimed to have a black belt in a martial art and began to land flying kicks on the front door causing the heavy door to shudder violently. Even with thick bolts across the top and bottom, it was obvious that the door would not hold out for long. Tom would not be dissuaded or calmed, even by the mention of the police.

Eventually, the hinges gave way and the substantial wooden door crashed into the entrance hall with Tom standing triumphantly on the other side of the threshold. It was the moment of truth. What were we to do now?

Ida was sitting halfway up the stairs to stop Tom from getting to Jim, and I was standing with Christina in the corridor by the door to the sitting room. Sue and Olaf were also in the corridor trying their best to get Tom to calm down. By this time David and Jean had arrived, and we were grateful for their calming influence. But Tom was still adamant he wasn't going to leave without the children.

Although not much more than five-feet tall, he was very powerfully built, and could likely cause us all great harm. It was going to take a minor miracle to get him out of the house and keep Ida and the children safe.

Two policemen eventually arrived and, seeing the damage, offered to arrest Tom and take him to the police station. David said he didn't think that would help, and so the police decided to give Tom a good talking to and then left. Although somewhat calmer now, he continued to try to get to Ida but was blocked by Jean sitting further down on the stairs.

With Tom and Ida shouting at each other the others tried to get them to communicate in a less confrontational way. Christina and I just stood where we were, praying silently and trying not to show our fear. I was feeling completely out of my depth and decided that it was better to let the more experienced adults try to end the stand-off.

Tom, however, remained unmoved. Realising that further violence would likely get him arrested, he changed tactics, threatening to take off all his clothes and sit on the corridor floor until we agreed to his terms. He was quite serious, presumably thinking that the ladies would be shocked into surrender. But they didn't back down, and it became clear that Tom was bluffing when he got down to his underpants and thought better of removing them.

But we still had a problem. The passage of time and the appearance of the police had calmed Tom, but we were at a stalemate with him refusing to leave, a gaping hole where the door once stood, and seemingly no way to persuade him to leave without inviting a violent reaction.

So he just sat himself down cross-legged by the door in his underpants while we waited. And he waited.

Thankfully it seemed he had given up trying to physically force Ida and the children to return to the flat with him. The issues then were: first, how to ensure Ida and the children stayed safe; second, how to get Tom out of the house; and third, how to help Tom and Ida constructively resolve their issues.

There was a long period of tense awkward silence.

It was now about two hours since Ida had come to the house. Tom started to complain that he had been misunderstood and unfairly treated ever since he was a child. He started talking about how he had been maltreated in a children's home and that no one could understand that. At this point I said that I had been in a children's home for most of my childhood. He looked surprised and turned to the others who nodded that it was indeed true. I then shared some of my feelings of abandonment, rejection, loneliness and fear of not amounting to anything. This seemed to connect with him, and he agreed to talk more with me on the way back to his flat. He also agreed that Ida and the children should stay at Sue and Olaf's for the night, and that he and Ida would accept help with their problems at a later date.

So Tom got dressed and we headed off into the dark and back to his flat, chatting about our experiences along the way. The walk to his flat in the cool outside air was a welcome relief from the tense claustrophobic stand-off. I remember drinking an almost neat glass of orange squash with Tom as he returned to his rational self, and then arriving back at Sue and Olaf's, feeling drained but relieved. I don't remember much after that. But the thought that stayed with me was that perhaps my childhood experiences could in some way be used for good after all. No one was more surprised by this than me.

This incident encouraged me to tell others about my background. As part of my All Nations responsibilities, I had been assigned to a local open youth club in the small nearby village of Stanstead Abbotts and so, when opportunities naturally arose, I shared parts of my story with the local teenagers. My student co-worker seemed fascinated by what I was saying, and I also had opportunities to share in my college worship group which met each morning for worship, prayer, Bible study and personal sharing. I was surprised that some members of the group had tears in their eyes when I shared my story. I didn't really understand why my story was having this impact, but I began to realise that it was more powerful than I had thought.

I was of course still carrying with me the emotional 'baggage' of that story.

Chapter 23

'Olandah'

I continued to visit my mother very occasionally at St Augustine's and to receive notifications from the mental health tribunal each time they declined my mother's appeals to be released from the hospital. There was no question that my mother was seriously ill and would need residential care for the foreseeable future and possibly for her entire lifetime. Sometimes during my visits she would either not recognise me or would be largely uncommunicative. But despite the discouraging nature of those visits, I persevered: I was, after all, probably the only visitor she had. But she remained largely a stranger who happened to be my mother. My grandmother was also a stranger to me having, as I have said, taken little interest in me at all. But it was while I was in my first year at All Nations that I got to know a lot more about her. Because in April 1987 she unexpectedly died.

The official-looking letter notifying me of her death was from a firm of solicitors based in the seaside town of Broadstairs where my grandmother Jean had lived for many years. It informed me that she had died, and that because of my mother's mental incapacity I was the legal executor. I was further informed that I should arrange for my gran's flat to be cleared of its possessions as soon as possible so that the tenancy could be terminated. I discussed this with my tutor, Vera, and explained to her that my gran had made a living from the occult and that it was likely that her flat contained occult objects that I would not want my relatives or anyone else to retrieve. Rather, I wanted those items retrieved and taken to a dump and destroyed before my own eyes. But I knew I would need help identifying these objects, and Vera suggested a certain Pastor Andy, who led a house church in the St Lawrence area of Ramsgate not far from Broadstairs.

So I arranged to meet Pastor Andy at the local dump where he showed me the things he had retrieved from the flat. These included tarot cards, a crystal ball and other occult objects that I would never have recognised as such: they all instinctively repelled me. Andy had already destroyed some of the things, but others like the crystal ball and the statuettes needed burying at the dump. So we asked a bulldozer driver to bury them while we watched. In this way I was satisfied that they could never be retrieved or used by anyone else.

It turned out that Pastor Andy knew of my grandmother. He told me that whenever she saw him walking towards her along the street in Broadstairs she would cross to the opposite pavement and snarl at him as she passed by. He quite rightly thought that this was bizarre behaviour and that she clearly disliked him. But apart from that, he had no other dealings with her. I didn't know what to make of her behaviour either except to conclude that she saw Andy as some kind of threat.

My grandmother's life was shaped by family tragedy, by failed personal relationships and later by her fascination with the occult. This dominated her life during her time in Broadstairs up until her untimely death there.

She changed her name to 'Olandah', practising as a clairvoyant from her small booth on the seafront frequented by tourists. She was well known locally for two things. The first was that each morning without fail she would walk down to a particular spot on the seafront to feed bread to the pigeons. She appears to have been very fond of animals and to my knowledge cared for a partially blind white poodle, a cat, a parrot and an injured raven in her very cramped flat. She had, however, a specific reason for feeding the pigeons: she was convinced that the love of her life Gypsy Lee had been reincarnated as one of them. I, amongst others, expressed real doubts about this, but she remained steadfast.

She was also well known for conducting readings using tarot cards, tea leaves, the palm of the hand and a crystal ball. These were mainly provided for curious tourists prepared to part with their cash. But Jean also conducted private seances, and among her clients were celebrities such as the actor Jack Warner from the BBC television series *Dixon of Dock Green*. She occasionally featured in the local newspaper and also had a small but devoted following across the UK.

But according to her sister Brenda, my grandmother could also act in very unloving ways towards my mother, and it is therefore unsurprising that Jean eventually placed Virginia into a children's home. Perhaps she recognised that she was not coping as a mother, or maybe she just wanted Virginia out of the way to ease her cramped living conditions and to allow her to continue unencumbered with her activities on the seafront.

The day of Gran's funeral arrived, and I was ambivalent about attending. I had wanted minimal involvement in the actual service and had heard that a local clergyman would officiate. But after speaking to him by phone, I was afraid he might try to excuse or explain away my gran's deep involvement in occultism. So I felt I needed in some way to express my deeply held view that occultism in all its forms was harmful and expressly prohibited by God. I felt I should do this because I genuinely wanted to prevent people being harmed. I would ideally have liked to have balanced this with some positive personal memories of my gran, but I simply had none to share. Instead, I encouraged the dozen or so mourners to listen to the voice of Jesus the Good Shepherd for themselves, to become one of his sheep and to be guided by him.

I was not left to do this on my own because Vera had kindly asked Kerr, a married student, to accompany me for moral support. He was the perfect choice, being kind and sympathetic throughout the entire day. Afterwards, I asked Kerr if I had been too hard on my gran, but he encouraged me, saying that what I had said was 'perfect'.

I felt further vindicated when an older lady asked to talk to me after the service. She was the owner of a local establishment, the Dundonald Hotel, and considered herself 'Olandah's best friend'. I noticed that several people referred to my gran as 'Olandah'. She said she was probably the last person to speak to my gran the night she died and thought I should know the details of what happened. The official cause of death was a heart attack, but this friend was sure that Jean's involvement in the occult had been responsible.

On the night of her death, Jean had phoned her in a terrified state. With great fear in her voice, she said, 'I can't control it anymore! It is out of control!' When her friend asked her what she meant, she replied, 'Things are flying across the room and the radio has burst into flames!' Those were her last words. This friend was clearly sad about the manner of Jean's passing. I have no reason to believe that she, a friend of my grandmother, would deliberately fabricate a story that would warn people away from what my grandmother believed and practised and describe my grandmother as a victim of evil. It simply served to confirm the existence of a power that was as malevolent as it was real.

My diary entry soon after the funeral service describes the difficulty I was having in understanding how my grandmother could have willingly engaged in such practices. Part of my diary entry for 12th May reads as follows:

My overriding feeling is one of sadness that yet another soul has gone to hell and I feel guilty that perhaps with a little more effort I could have brought her to faith in Jesus. I saw her as an active collaborator with Satan. Now, in the light of comments made about her by friends and acquaintances it seems as if she may simply have been the unconscious victim of satanic activity – she dabbled a little, and a little was enough to get her trapped e.g. the uncontrollable spontaneous combustion. Walking through the college's surrounding greenery I wept briefly for my gran. God is loving and merciful but cannot let sin pass unjudged. The death and resurrection of Jesus the Son of God show us how God reconciles the reality of evil [with] the need for justice and offers forgiveness and eternal life to all who put their trust in Jesus. As far as I knew, my gran had placed her [ultimate] trust elsewhere.

At funerals you are struck by the finality of death. What has been done can no longer be undone. Neither can that which has been left undone, be completed. The consequences are stark, and the choice, ours.

I had gradually been convinced of the reality of such evil by the teaching and practice of Christian leaders such as John Wimber. Their deliverance ministry powerfully demonstrated the reality of those evil forces but also the victory of Christ over them. It was wonderful to see the transformation of people after their deliverance.

The following year I purchased Michael Green's book *I Believe in Satan's Downfall* which is for me the best book written on the subject of evil for a general readership. Around the same time I got talking about this subject to another student in my year called Chris. He was now in his early 40s but as a young man had been deeply involved in astrology and he gladly told me his story.

Due to tragic family circumstances which left him traumatised and fatherless as a very young child, Chris grew up feeling rejected and inferior. As a young man he had been fascinated by the supernatural and started studying astrology. After a while he found that he could sometimes predict in detail what was going to happen to specific individuals, and so he immersed himself more and more deeply into the occult as it gave him the power and significance he had lacked growing up. But there was a price to be paid too. He was increasingly disturbed by very lifelike nightmares featuring strange and terrible beasts that tormented and terrified him and against which he felt powerless. He felt he was being dragged deeper and deeper into something over which he had no control. In short, he had become a victim of the occult powers he had used to help him deal with his childhood experiences. He tried turning to the Bible for help but each time he opened it, the pages blinded him with brilliant white light, forcing him to slam it shut. Eventually, he decided to ask for help from a local church leader in West Bridgford, Nottingham. After many months of struggle, which involved renouncing the devil and all his works and trusting in Christ, the nightmares became less frequent and terrifying until he was able finally and completely to break free. And now he was studying at All Nations to pursue his calling to work cross-culturally. Chris went on to have a powerful ministry, and his life was living proof of the transforming power of Christ. Had he not told me his story I would never have guessed just how deeply he had been enmeshed in occultism.

Chris's testimony also helped me understand both the incident in the underground waiting room and Pastor Andy's encounters with my gran. Chris told me that at the height of his involvement in occultism, he could identify individual Christians as they passed him on the street. He said it was nothing to do with their physical appearance, but rather that they were surrounded by a white aura which non-Christians did not have. That realisation was a cause for concern but also a cause for celebration. As Spirit-filled Christians we are to be aware of the power of occultism but more than that to celebrate the truth that 'He that is in us is greater than he who is in the world'![3] My grandmother's tragic and untimely death and Chris's testimony both reinforced that conviction.

I found myself developing a better theological understanding of my faith, but not without hardships. My diary reveals that I was finding it tough going having to study four subjects in depth in just 20 hours per week. No wonder I was worrying that I wouldn't achieve diploma level, and I wasn't the only one struggling. It wasn't until the second year that I found some helpful study strategies.

I was also struggling with my relationship with Christina. It had started well but by June 1987 I was having doubts about our compatibility. Once again I found myself wanting to end a relationship as gently as I could, but I didn't know how. As it was, my first-year exams would preoccupy me until early July so I couldn't do anything until then. Perhaps my upcoming six-week placement in Indonesia would give me time to think . . .

Chapter 24

Indonesia

I had never been abroad in my life. Never.

So when I came to choose where I would go for the mandatory six-week cross-cultural placement I decided to make the most of it. I had been impressed and intrigued by Martin Goldsmith's tales about the churches of Indonesia and the need for more missionaries. And as the largest Muslim nation in the world Indonesia aligned with my sense of calling.

Thus it was that in late July 1987 I found myself on a KLM flight to the Indonesian capital, Jakarta. It was not so much a flight, but rather a seemingly unending conveyor belt of in-flight food. But I wasn't complaining, and it made the 20-hour flight a lot more bearable.

The first thing I noticed on leaving the air-conditioned comfort of the plane at Jakarta airport was the wall of heat and humidity that engulfed me. I realised then that this was going to be very different to anything I had experienced before, and I couldn't help feeling slightly insecure. I was comforted by the timely appearance of my hosts, and within an hour or so I was sitting at a dining table at the Jakarta offices of the Overseas Missionary Fellowship (OMF).

I had hardly slept at all during the flight and hadn't been able to take in any of the sights, sounds and smells during the drive from the airport. So I was looking forward to a lengthy rest. On entering the guest bedroom I realised that this might be quite a challenge. For one thing, there was no air-conditioning, and the ceiling fan simply moved the warm, humid air around the room rather than cooling it significantly. The bed was framed by a mosquito net and the air was heavily impregnated with the pungent smell of mosquito spray. I was aware that malaria was a real problem in Indonesia, and although I was taking the prescribed prophylactics, I was grateful for the net protection. In addition, I quickly realised that my bed was only a stone's throw away from a noisy six-lane arterial road that seemed to carry the capital's traffic most of the night and day. But that first day I could have slept through anything, so I gratefully accepted the invitation to put my head down for a couple of hours.

I spent two weeks in Jakarta during which time my body gradually adjusted to the jetlag but I still found myself at times lying on my bed at 3am wide awake. During this time in Jakarta, I was gradually introduced to the local OMF staff: a mixture of British, Swiss, American and German nationals aided by some local people.

My guide in Jakarta was a German missionary who introduced me to the delights of the city. Jakarta was, and still is, a city of almost unimaginable contrasts. On the one hand are the symbols of great wealth and power: the shiny international bank buildings and hotels, the presidential palace and the Indonesian parliamentary campuses. On the other, there is grinding poverty with extended families living in bamboo and tin shacks propped over stinking black drainage channels or built within inches of busy railway tracks. There was the constant roar of traffic, the whining of the ubiquitous moped, and beggars old and very young at busy road junctions thrusting out their malnourished hands every time the traffic lights turned red.

My German guide impressed me by taking it all in his stride and always giving the beggars some money. To me they were a nuisance; to him they were poor and needed all the help they could get. I also saw this compassion illustrated by an older female missionary working in a labyrinthine *kampung* (village) area of the city. She had lived in Indonesia for decades, teaching English and basic health education to some of the poorest people in Jakarta. She wore very plain clothes and tied up her grey hair in a bun. And she lived very simply in a clean if sparsely furnished one-bedroom *kampung* dwelling with a small, enclosed patio garden which she tended with great care and devotion.

I helped move her furniture into her new dwelling while the locals looked on with interest, asking many questions which she answered in fluent colloquial Indonesian. The locals were clearly very excited about having a Westerner in their midst and appreciated what she would contribute to their community. I was impressed by her sacrifice and commitment but also by her obvious love for these people. I was also challenged, wondering if I could ever make a similar commitment.

OMF had other workers located throughout Indonesia, and I was able to visit some of them too. One of them was Gerald, a Dutch-born Canadian missionary teaching at the reformed seminary in a hilltop town called Tomohon, in the Minahasa sub-district of North Sulawesi. I was supposed to be staying with him and his wife, but she had returned urgently to Canada at very short notice, leaving Gerald to take responsibility for me and my programme.

The aeroplane trip to Manado, the provincial capital of Minahasa, was memorable for several reasons. First, there was the plane, a twin-engine propeller-driven model flown by a domestic travel firm called Bouraq which looked like it had seen better days. I really wondered if we'd survive the trip, but at the half-way point when we landed in the eastern Borneo city of Balikpapan to refuel, I started to believe that I would in fact arrive safely. The food on board was delicious, a spicy rice-based dish followed by an exotic fruit cocktail of lychees, pineapple and rambutan (literally, 'hairy one'). One lasting memory is the continuous stream of cigarette smoke drifting towards me in the tail section throughout the entire journey. It had a curious smell, very different from Western cigarette smoke, due to the added ingredient: cloves. These, I was to learn, were a very valuable Minahasan export to many parts of the world.

After counting innumerable fluffy white clouds dotted across the brilliant blue sky and dozens of small tropical islands planted in the shining turquoise sea, I breathed a sigh of relief as the single tarmac runway came into view.

Gerald greeted me and drove me up the winding road to his home in the cool mountain town of Tomohon. He had devised a programme of activities which took me to various parts of Minahasa. These included a tour of local churches and children's groups led by a church elder called Pak Billy (named after Billy Graham) and meetings at the Bethesda Christian Hospital to review the role of the church in promoting primary healthcare. I also had a memorable visit to a very remote village to see that healthcare in action.

The Indonesians and Westerners I met greatly inspired me with their sacrificial love and practical help for the Minahasan people. I had much to learn! And there were also some very definite benefits to living and working in Tomohon with its friendly people, cooler mountain air and beautiful setting. But on the return journey, gazing out of the Bouraq plane window, I wasn't at all sure that I would be returning to Tomohon or indeed to anywhere else in Indonesia. For one thing, I couldn't see that I had anything of value to contribute; and for another, I wasn't sure whether I had what it took to work cross-culturally.

I had felt homesick throughout my time in Indonesia. Each day as I tuned into the shortwave BBC World Service broadcasts I felt the comforting tug of the familiar. I had learned so much, but I also longed to return home to recuperate. The language and cultural differences left me disorientated and uncertain about what was going on and how I should respond in most situations. I was also trying to cope with the hot and humid climate and with being on a completely different continent half a world away. I felt quite helpless, having to rely completely on others because of my inability to communicate and my inexperience and ignorance of how things worked in Indonesia. The name for this is 'culture shock', a common experience for anyone who finds themselves devoid of familiar reference points. This phase typically lasts between six and 24 months, and some people handle it with ease, while others find it much more difficult. Some indeed never make the transition. I would put myself into the category of those who find it more difficult to adjust than most. The OMF staff had clearly adjusted many years before, and they were now very comfortable living and working in Indonesia. But I wasn't at all sure I could make the same adjustment.

After a final sweaty, sleepless night at the OMF headquarters, I waved farewell to my hosts and headed eagerly for the air-conditioned luxury of the KLM cabin. I was glad to be going home where I could unwind in familiar surroundings and, in time, take stock of all that I had experienced. And that, of course, was the main purpose of the placement.

Chapter 25

Else

And take stock, I did.

My diary entries in the days before resuming my All Nations studies show that my Indonesian experience had caused me to doubt my calling and suitability as a missionary, and that my time away had done nothing to allay my growing doubts about my relationship with Christina.

These entries clearly show my despair at yet again choosing an incompatible potential marriage partner. I felt bad that I had not taken the time to get to *really know* her well before committing to the relationship. The diary indicates that these doubts had been triggered by a pastoral studies (PCC) lecture entitled 'Broken Homes' that stirred some deep and unresolved personal insecurities connected to my childhood and so I conclude *I do not know what to look for in an imagined partner because I've not seen or been a part of a model marriage.* So these doubts were rooted in my own unresolved issues. The PCC lectures were designed to achieve two goals: to provide us with basic pastoral insights about the best way to help others and to gently help us understand our own issues. I found those lectures so helpful that I would have chosen to attend All Nations for them alone. However, it was only after leaving that I found people who could help me receive God's transformational healing.

At that time I did not fully appreciate that my difficulties with the opposite sex and with discerning God's leading were directly related to deep-seated unresolved issues. I genuinely desired to do God's will but wasn't sure if that would mean marriage or singleness for me. So, in order to clarify my thoughts, I drew up a list of seven issues and their pros and cons. These were: financial security, companionship, ministry together, decision-making, a settled home, children, and the probability of this being God's will for me. I concluded that for me *being single is the greater challenge because it would entail a greater reliance on faith and God's promises in the face of having no home or means of support*. I found some inspiration from the example of Abraham, recognising that I needed to hear God's voice as he did: *the only reason he moved was because God told him to, not because it benefited him materially or otherwise: he walked by faith*. But by then I had enough self-insight to realise that unless I was convinced of God's goodness and benevolence, I was more likely to be motivated by fear than by joyful obedience.

I wrestled with my missionary calling and decided to pose the question: *how much choice does the Lord give me in these things?* I started by listing my doubts: a fair complexion which burns easily and attracts mosquitoes; a body that I don't think can take *a dose of the more serious diseases*, and years of language study. I then asked, *are these excuses?* And then I considered the benefits of not being a missionary: work to be done in the UK, *certain Byron wants me to stay at Calvary to lead the youth work.*

Also, *I need stability and a family*. Conclusion? *I'm not sure that becoming a missionary would give me these*. So *I need to stay in Britain if I am to have full benefits of stability and a family*. Then I returned to the critical question, *is this what the Lord wants for me though?* At that point I concluded, *I think that he is giving me a free hand – it's up to me in the absence of any guidance to the contrary*.

But the next sentence in my diary indicates that it is my deep and unmet needs for stability and companionship that are most strongly influencing me. *I think that it's time I settle down and put some roots down, and the best way for me to do that is to stay in Britain*. I was not ruling out full-time Christian work in Britain, but I clearly wasn't at all ready to serve overseas while my underlying issues were unresolved.

I recommenced All Nations in mid-September and after a couple of weeks Christina and I agreed to end the relationship. This lifted one very real pressure, but I had other pressing issues to attend to: my studies, lobbying to be elected the senior male student and trying to sort out a £1,400 shortfall in my finances caused by a change in circumstances for one of my supporters. Once again I approached John Honey, and once again the Trustees agreed to meet this financial need. This was all the more remarkable because Spurgeon's was at that time still adjusting to a completely new social care model and was running a deficit of £100,000. In return, I wrote a short article for *Within Our Gates*, the Spurgeon's magazine, with the title 'From Birchington to Sulawesi'. In it I described my experiences in Minahasa and explained how Spurgeon's support had enabled me to attend All Nations.

But I continued to struggle with the demands of study and college life. All of this wasn't helped by several days of enforced bed rest at the beginning of October due to a badly strained back. Then on the night of 15th October the whole of the UK was battered by a hurricane which felled swathes of trees, damaged buildings and caused widespread power failures. All Nations was plunged into darkness, and we carried on as best we could with candles and alternative forms of heating for two nights.

On the second evening I was lying on the couch in the front entrance hall where other students were seated. With candles dotted around the hall and up the grand staircase, it was a rather cosy and intimate setting. At that point, it became even more intimate and cosy when a female student called Else came across and sat by me for a chat. I don't know why she approached me, because at that time I was in a bad place physically and emotionally. My back was very painful and only very slowly improving, and I was still working through the emotional aftermath of Christina. In addition, my acne had flared up badly and I had grown a beard partly to try to cover it and partly as a reflection of my depressed emotional state: my diary describes it as *a grey mood* that I couldn't shake off. It didn't help that the beard made me look like an old sea captain rather than a handsome and intelligent young man . . . Else by contrast had spent her six-week placement in Israel and had developed a healthy tan, making her much more attractive.

Whatever her reasons for talking to me, my appearance didn't put her off and we spent the whole evening chatting very easily. Later that night I found myself reflecting on that, and on the fact that she was an exceptionally good listener. Up to that point, all I knew about her was that she had spent the year before All Nations training as a church worker at the rapidly growing Ichthus Christian Fellowship (ICF) in south-east London, led by Roger Forster. The man who had impressed me at Spring Harvest just over a year before.

One thing that Else and I had very much in common was our conviction that God was again working through signs and wonders and spiritual gifts. I had witnessed God doing so at Calvary, and although he hadn't used me directly in this way, I made it clear to others that this is what I believed.

Then one day and quite unexpectedly a new first-year student (whom I shall call Jenny) asked me if God had ever used me in healing. I was taken aback but couldn't stop myself saying 'yes' – with no intent to deceive. This was obviously the answer she was looking for as she then asked me if I would pray for her heel. She had badly injured it while horse-riding, and it had developed a large growth which prevented her from wearing her normal shoes. So would I pray for it? Forced into a corner, my reply was a hesitant 'yes', but with one condition. I said it would be better if a group of us prayed. This might increase the likelihood of success, and it would take time to get such a group together. More than anything, though, it was my way of sharing the 'blame' if (as I thought likely) the healing failed to materialise.

The appointed day came and about five of us surrounded Jenny. We prayed for several minutes, after which there was absolutely no visible change to Jenny's heel. I repeated that sometimes healing happens in stages or isn't immediately apparent and so on. She thanked us warmly and, as we dispersed, I felt that I'd managed to retrieve the situation without too much personal embarrassment.

The following morning, Jenny excitedly told me that her heel was back to normal, with no sign of the growth. She was clearly elated. By contrast, my internal response was, 'I can't believe it! Is she just trying to be encouraging?' But overall I felt tremendously relieved that God had overruled to Jenny's benefit. Of course, to this day I don't know if God used me or another member of the group to heal Jenny. But it taught me to be humbler about my own abilities, and to be much more ready to give the glory to God.

Then as now it was my earnest desire to do God's will. But perhaps I was overthinking it – making it more complicated than it was and setting my sights hopelessly high. On 3rd December, a week before the end of the autumn term, I wrote out in my diary several lines from Bonhoeffer's *The Cost of Discipleship* based on Mark chapter 2 verse 14, the calling of Levi (Matthew). The parts I underlined in my entry are:

> *[He leaves all that he has] but not because he thinks that he might be doing something worthwhile . . . He is called out, and has to forsake his old life . . . The old life is left behind, and completely surrendered.*[4]

Despite my earlier decision to stay in the UK for companionship and security, I was still not sure that this was in line with God's will. I had no peace. I was also finding Else increasingly attractive, wondering if she might feature in God's plans for me. But I couldn't be sure that she was interested in me, and two other male students also seemed very friendly towards Else and she towards them. If I was to get in before them, I had to act quickly. So I managed to engineer a lift with her to London and when the other passengers had both alighted I asked her if she would like to meet for a pizza sometime during the holiday. She agreed and drove off to stay with her friends Alan and Mary in Beckenham, south-east London.

We met at a local Pizza Hut, and things went very well. We continued where we had left off in the car, talking easily and enjoying each other's company. Despite my nervousness about starting yet another relationship and the prospect of failure, I was sufficiently impressed to summon up the courage to ask if we could meet again before Christmas Day. We agreed to meet at the National Gallery in central London, and before we parted I gave her a Christmas card and cardboard-framed picture as a Christmas present. I later learnt that this gesture was important to her because she was determined not to get her hopes up lest she be disappointed. We agreed to meet again the following day at Else's church and following this arranged to spend Christmas together at Else's family home.

The five-bedroom cottage in the centre of the ancient Oxfordshire village of Harwell was home to Else's mother Ursel. Else's brother Tom lived at home when he wasn't attending teacher training college, but the other adult children were living elsewhere. Her older brothers, Geoff and Andy, had married and lived locally with their children, and her younger sister Hanna was living in Leeds.

We arrived in the evening darkness. Tom introduced himself and we chatted easily in front of the fire in the main sitting room. He was clearly intrigued to find out more about his eldest sister's new boyfriend. The family and especially Else's mother put me completely at my ease, something which for me was so very important. I felt accepted and was therefore able to relax.

So on return to All Nations Else and I told people we were now in a relationship. Our happiness was, however, tempered by the pressures of college life and academic study. I found it increasingly difficult to spend quality time with Else due to unrelenting assignment deadlines and my senior student responsibilities, even with the senior female student Sarah doing so much on my behalf. Because of the tension that all this caused, we agreed to fix specific timeslots during the week when we could meet alone.

I found the pressure of the very full curriculum getting to me and the demands of local church ministry were substantially heavier during the second year. Added to this was my personal desire to get things just right, meaning that I spent far too much time preparing for these ministry opportunities. As it is, I don't believe that all that preparation led to much blessing. I remember one particular ministry opportunity that illustrated my talent for leaving things just too late.

It was at a well-known large church in Cambridgeshire. A group of about six of us arrived at the chapel on time and a fellow student, Dave R, preached a good sermon. I was due to preach at the evening service but was not at all prepared. Consequently, while the others enjoyed the hospitality of our hosts that afternoon, I frantically tried (unsuccessfully) to finish my sermon in a separate room. The evening service approached and I was in a highly anxious and stressed state. I intended to preach from the first part of Ephesians chapter 4: as it was, it was a complete disaster and probably best forgotten, except that it is a memory that keeps me humble.

Much of it was a rehashed version of a technical commentary on Ephesians which my hearers probably found exceedingly boring, and by the end I had succeeded in questioning the congregation's lack of love and unity. I could feel myself digging a deeper and deeper hole, but I was powerless to stop myself. It was a great relief all round when I finally ground to a halt 20 minutes over the allotted time. The worst part came at the end of the service when I stood at the door to thank people for coming and they me. They were polite but their appreciation was very muted. My fellow students were also unimpressed and hardly spoke to me during the awkward one-hour return journey. I tried to excuse my behaviour as 'trying to be prophetic', but they weren't convinced any more than I was! I knew that my lack of preparation and anxiety were the main reasons for this highly embarrassing episode. And yet I had thought that this would be a golden opportunity to parade my learning and impress others. There was, however, one ray of light in the midst of this seemingly impenetrable darkness.

Before leaving the church, I had made my way to the front of the sanctuary to collect my thoughts and to avoid any potentially awkward conversations. So I was surprised when a bespectacled scholarly 40-year-old man approached me with an outstretched hand, saying, 'You certainly put a lot of work into that!' I didn't quite know how to respond except to say, 'Yes, I did.' In retrospect he probably also meant that I had gone on for far too long! Thankfully he didn't dwell on that but instead asked me what my plans were after All Nations. I told him that I hoped to pursue further theological study, at which point he revealed that he taught theology at Cambridge University, and that he was sure he could get me in on the back of his coat tails. I had no idea what that meant and it raised questions in my mind. Who would pay? Where would I stay? But it was clear that he saw potential in me that no one else did – least of all myself. His name was Hugh W, and I learnt much later that he was a lecturer in Hebrew and Aramaic, with impressive academic credentials. When I did later discover his identity, it meant a great deal to me that in the aftermath of an awful sermon, he saw past that to what I could be and was willing to help me get there. It was an extraordinary gesture of grace and kindness.

As it happened, I again failed by the narrowest of margins to get the exam results I needed to pursue further studies. In any case, I had by that time realised that I simply wasn't gifted enough to pursue further studies and so I wouldn't be taking up Hugh's offer. That door had closed, but where was I to look for an open one?

Interestingly enough, my March 1987 diary entry a year earlier shows that I had foreseen this eventuality. I had been afraid I would end up leaving college with no job and no permanent home to go to. So I was always trying to think ahead to avoid being penniless and homeless. At that point, there were three main things that preoccupied me: my relationship with Christina, whether I achieved a certificate or diploma, and the availability of paid ministry openings in the UK or overseas. I now knew the answer to the first two questions and continued to commit my future to the Lord despite my powerful underlying fears.

But even with this greater sense of clarity I still found it incredibly difficult to leave All Nations. It was so painful that I wept uncontrollably when it came time to say goodbye to my fellow students. No matter how much I tried I was powerless to stop myself weeping. This was shocking to me but, in retrospect, it was, like my anger, an overreaction triggered by unresolved deep-seated personal pain rooted in my childhood. Even after two years at All Nations, I was still carrying a lot of emotional baggage from my childhood.

Chapter 26

Score-draw

On leaving All Nations we decided that Else would return to London and I to Cardiff to find work while we considered what God had for us next. This was by no means clear. Else was able to find employment as a dietitian, while I had to settle for a temporary clerical job after which Calvary offered me the position of casual labourer to help complete the rebuilding of the church hall. However, it didn't take me long to discover that all was not well at Calvary. There were some important relationship difficulties but I felt that there was little that I could do to help.

By contrast, my relationship with Else was deepening significantly, and my diary shows me asking *is she the one?* I was still grappling with two of the three key issues I had previously identified in March 1987: future ministry and singleness/marriage. As before, I found that it helped clarify my thinking to write them down in question form:

1. *In marrying Else, am I also 'marrying' Ichthus?*

2. *If I'm no longer called to Muslims and/or Ichthus, will Else still marry me?*

3. *How does Else see headship of a husband vis-a-vis his wife?*

In other words, should we get married if we don't have a clear joint vision? I recalled that one of our respected All Nations lecturers had advised that pursuing a relationship was more important than compatibility of calling, since that calling could change for a variety of reasons. The same was true of our clear theological understandings of the husband-wife relationship. Over and above those considerations, I felt very hesitant about how well I could handle the responsibilities of marriage. But even with those reservations and worries I felt that the Lord had given me a free hand – the choice is mine whether or not to marry Else. So on the morning of 26th December 1988 while staying at Harwell for Christmas I proposed to Else and she accepted. My next diary entry on 10th January describes my feelings:

> I got engaged to her on 26th December 1988. It wasn't premeditated, it just happened naturally! I'm sure it's the right decision and the right timing because even looking back at some of my reasons for holding back (mainly looking at my own ability to face up to the responsibilities of a husband and a father) they aren't now an issue – they've not been suppressed, they simply evaporated.

Engagement took the tension out of our relationship. Else had waited patiently, without really understanding why I was taking so much time to make up my mind. Now we could start to plan for our wedding and set some joint goals. One of them was that I'll be moving to London when I get a job and accommodation. That decision had not been an easy one. But it is worth retelling in detail how it came about because it was a clear example of how the Lord tended to speak into my life and direct me.

By December I had finally concluded that I was unlikely to be offered a paid ministry role at Calvary. It was nothing personal, it was just that Calvary had changed. Nonetheless, I still felt I might possibly play a part in helping the church through these changes and so wanted to stay. I had been putting out feelers for jobs with my old employer and received a provisional offer to start in medical personnel in the new year, on the same salary and grade as before. Although the salary and job security were attractive and meant I could stay in Cardiff, I also wanted confirmation from the Lord. All I knew at the time was that I didn't want to move to London unless I really had to. Not only would I lose all that I had in Cardiff, but I was convinced from what I had already experienced of Ichthus over the past few months that I would hate it . . .

I liked to think that I had never been one to 'cop out' and avoid thinking and praying through difficult and uncomfortable issues. But, if God wanted me to move to London, then he would have to make that very clear to me. So, I began with my preferred method of writing down the questions and issues, listing the advantages of moving to London in one column and the advantages of staying in Cardiff in the other. I tried to be as honest as I could, and then added up the totals for each option. That was logical and rational enough, I felt, except that the totals were quite unexpectedly the same for both columns! While wondering what on earth to do next, the following thoughts entered my mind: 'It's right for you to move to London. You won't like it, but it will do you good.' It's true that I didn't like that thought, but I couldn't deny that it had a ring of truth and authority to it, reminiscent of the insight I had had three years earlier in the Pearl Assurance building. It certainly couldn't have been auto-suggestion because I really didn't want to go to London. But I couldn't deny that it was a clear answer to my question, and I felt I had to honour it. I remember sitting there thinking, 'I don't like this answer. But I know it is right.'

I don't remember much about my Calvary farewells except acknowledging to myself and some close friends that my time there had been a blessing in so many ways, especially the hospitality and warm fellowship. Byron's anointed leadership had been another factor, and his preaching and the friendship of Colin and Lynette had helped me extricate myself from the unsuitable relationship with Denise and set me on the road to All Nations. Three and a half years on from that, I was engaged and about to marry someone who was the answer to my prayers. The question, 'Who, if anyone, am I going to marry?' had been answered. I had arrived in Cardiff with so many doubts about what I believed. Calvary's openness to the supernatural activity of the Holy Spirit helped me work through those doubts, convincing me that God was real and providing a legitimate and satisfying alternative to the traditionalism of my childhood. I had arrived with questions such as, 'What is God really like?' and 'Is there more to Christianity than this?' These had now largely been answered.

I also felt that my questions about money, career and family had been resolved. I had long dreaded the prospect of getting to retirement and only then realising that I had invested myself in the wrong things. Martin Goldsmith had once remarked in a sermon that when Jesus said, 'Where your treasure is, your heart will be also',[5] he wasn't saying it was wrong to have a treasure, but that we should ensure that it was the *right* treasure. For me, my treasure had shifted from material and emotional security to seeking God's will for my life above all else. Although I was sad to leave my Cardiff friends, I could at least take comfort knowing that we were agreed that moving to London was indeed God's next step for me.

Even with that conviction, the transition was not going to be easy. In mid-March, in order to prepare for what was to come, I spent a few days in an Anglican retreat house, fasting and praying to further discern God's will. I received no specific guidance about God's plans for which organisation we should join or where we were to serve overseas.

On 16th March I wrote:

> *If I **am** asking for too much in advance, then what are the underlying reasons for this presumption? What's wrong with asking God about which country and which organisation he wants to send us to and with? It is all very well for people to say 'wait' but that doesn't seem to be a **reason** to do so.*

What I didn't realise at the time was that I *was* asking for too much in advance and that there were several important reasons why we *should* wait. But one thing I did begin to realise during that retreat was that I was in effect very subtly trying to manipulate God:

*Too often I **don't** trust God and I don't have faith in him to bless me, so I try to manipulate him into a situation where I say, 'Well, I've given this up for you (e.g. fasting for a few days) so, in all fairness you ought to give me something in return!'*

I was able to conclude that this was a lesson in faith, and I took comfort in the words of Romans 8:28 that God would work everything out. Well, at least eventually. I also found comfort in the Old Testament figures of Moses, Joshua and Isaiah who lived out that life of faith.

As usual I had been badly overthinking issues when I should instead have relaxed and kept things simple. So it was a tremendous encouragement when towards the end of the retreat, as I was praying, I felt God gently reassure me, 'It's going to be all right.' God graciously gave me the peace to be able to rest in that assurance.

Chapter 27

Ichthus

Just a month later I was living in a shared terraced house located in the Peckham area of south-east London. Else was only a ten-minute walk away, lodging with three friends from her former church in north London. All of them held leadership positions in Ichthus. At that time, Ichthus numbered over a thousand members and was growing rapidly. People throughout London and the UK were attracted by Roger's clear biblical teaching, openness to the work of the Holy Spirit, advocacy of female leadership, and commitment to church planting.

On the face of it, there was much to attract me too. But, as the Lord had forewarned me, I didn't like it at all. I remember rationalising the move to London by saying to myself and slightly tongue in cheek: 'I am a missionary to Ichthus.' I wanted to change Ichthus but, as I was to discover, the Lord had other plans.

I was also struggling with the loss of friends, the loss of employment and worrying about a small overdraft and the plans for our forthcoming wedding in August. And I was also conscious that I lacked any sense of focus or direction. I was not in a good place.

But I struggled on, and eventually secured a temporary clerical post in the housing benefits section of Southwark Council. It was another boring job made somewhat interesting by the unique and at times thoroughly eccentric characters who worked there and who would have made a valuable case study about the sociology of work. A few weeks later I was offered the post of Senior HR Officer at Newham Council in east London.

The job at Newham came just at the right time. It was at a level of seniority similar to my peers which restored my sense of self-esteem. And the salary eliminated any worries about how we were going to finance our wedding. I was also looking forward to having our own privacy and putting some distance between us and what I called at the time 'Cowerbridge shop'. This referred to the gossip between people who attended the small Ichthus congregation in a primary school in the district of what I shall call Cowerbridge. The congregation was led by Steve and Jill, old friends of Else's from her previous church. I was not a great fan, and one of my diary entries at the time shows why:

> I have got very little (very very little!) out of the
> Cowerbridge or Ichthus Central activities since I've
> been in London . . . And I have no vision of my own
> with which to contribute.

I found myself seeking God's presence directly, basing that approach on Hebrews 10:19-23, and hoping that this would help me find clarity and the ability to overcome these difficulties.

This was of course very difficult for Else. She loved Ichthus, having positive memories of her full-time training year only three years before. She also valued her friendship with Steve and Jill and knew that if we were to leave and look for another congregation, they would inevitably take this personally. Besides that, she was sharing a house with them, and it was likely that we would live there immediately after we married while we looked for accommodation of our own. I therefore resigned myself to waiting for at least several months more. But I wasn't at all happy: I didn't feel that my gifts were appreciated, or that I was given opportunities to use them. What I didn't realise then was that I was being perceived by some as unsupportive, overcritical and arrogant. In this they were right.

Still, I found satisfaction in my new job. I was working in the HR section dealing with non-teaching staff employed by the education department. My job was to ensure that all personnel matters were properly dealt with by my team of six. I had been interviewed by Trevor, the overall boss, and offered the job there and then. I found out later that Trevor was a leader in a local church and was familiar with All Nations. I also discovered that he hadn't appointed me simply because I was a Christian and I was glad about that: the deciding factors were that I met the selection criteria and . . . I happened to be the sole applicant. This was rather a surprise to me: perhaps God was in this more than I thought. The work was relatively straightforward and not at all stressful. The weeks flew by until one morning I arrived at work to find my work area bedecked with decorations and presents wishing me well for my upcoming marriage, then only a few days away. I was completely bowled over by this demonstration of kindness from people I had only just got to know, and it set me up for the biggest day of my life.

Chapter 28

Life Together

Else took the main responsibility for planning and organising our wedding day. We had decided to reduce costs by keeping the reception simple. Even so, we ended up with a guest list of 120, and so it was still going to be a huge task. Several members of the Cowerbridge congregation generously offered to help with serving tables, and one of the ladies, a professional caterer, played an indispensable part in making our day a huge success. Perhaps being part of Ichthus had its benefits after all?

The day itself was hot and sunny. Phil D, one of my friends from All Nations, had agreed to be my best man. We arrived in a bit of a rush but had a couple of minutes to compose ourselves and hurried down the aisle to sit on the front pew, greatly relieved to have got to the church on time! But we needn't have worried. With the help of Trixie, her chief bridesmaid, Else took all the time she needed to look her very best before entering the sanctuary. After all, this was her big day as much as it was mine.

I took time to look around the church sanctuary. The building itself had been rebuilt in 1959 as the Dietrich Bonhoeffer Memorial Church and Ichthus was renting it from the Lutheran Church as the location for its main Sunday morning congregational service.

From the outside, an observer would see a largely unprepossessing utilitarian light-brick building. But inside, the light-brown beech and oak interior was beautifully complemented by the brilliant sunshine streaming through the tall stained-glass windows close to where we were sitting. These windows were like vivid glass paintings and their colourful vibrancy reflected my mood of joy and excitement. This was further heightened by the presence of friends from Cardiff and All Nations. The building was packed. But what meant most to me was the presence of Mary, June and Mike, and John: these dear people had been there with me through it all. I felt that this was the culmination of all their efforts on my behalf over many years. I was now 29 years old, and they had each in their own way made this day possible. For me, this day was as much a tribute to them as anything else, and I hoped very much that they would also see it that way.

The moment of truth approached as the organ heralded the entrance of the bride. The congregation rose to acknowledge her. I waited for a few moments but eventually turned my head to see my beautiful bride coming towards me. Accompanying her were her elder brother Geoffrey, Trixie with Rachel and Sam, Else's niece and nephew as bridesmaid and page boy. Else looked so radiantly beautiful that I struggled to hold the tears back. I was absolutely elated, and Else looked very happy but as calm and composed as I had ever seen her.

The service was over very quickly. Steve from Cowerbridge married us, Phil produced the rings at the right time, Byron preached, Calvary folk performed musical pieces for us, and the congregation sang their hearts out.

By the time we had made our way back up the aisle as man and wife to sign the register, the whole thing was a blur. But I do remember catching the eye of great-aunt Brenda and her daughter Sandra: they had kindly brought my mother along to be part of the day. I'm not sure what she made of it all because apart from congratulating us she said very little. I believe she was probably trying to keep herself together as much as anything. She wasn't at all used to large gatherings, and the support of Brenda, Sandra and Else's mum Ursel at the reception probably helped her enter into our celebration in ways which would have otherwise been impossible.

The reception in the adjacent church hall was also memorable. Phil made an excellent best man's speech; Geoffrey did his bit as the senior male representative of Else's family; and the All Nations students sang a very entertaining song written by Phil based on the hymn 'Guide Me O Thou Great Redeemer'. The Calvary folk also did a turn, as did Else's Swiss aunt, Doris.

My speech was off-the-cuff because I wasn't really sure exactly what I wanted to say. I know I rambled, but I do remember thanking the Cowerbridge team for their much-needed help, and that the gist of my speech consisted of my heartfelt thanks to John, Mary, Mike, June, Maureen, Winnie and Calvary for getting me to this point in my life. It all seemed quite unbelievable to me and at times I felt lost for words, but I did my best and of course people were very appreciative.

By about 6:30pm it was all over. We got changed and drove away in Else's trusty Datsun Sunny to loud cheers, with the clanking of tins tied to the car bumper sending us on our way into married life and on to our honeymoon in Scotland for a couple of weeks.

The honeymoon was soon over and we returned to live in the top flat of a house occupied by Else's friends while we found somewhere suitable to rent. That was because we didn't have enough money to put down on a mortgage and were reluctant to put down roots until we knew what the future held. In the meantime, Else continued to work at Redbridge Health Authority and I at Newham Council. It helped that we could commute together, but the deeper question to which we did not have a clear answer was, 'What has God got in store for us?' This had not changed by mid-October:

> *I felt certain at one time that the Lord was calling me to work among ethnic minorities in this country. So much seems to have altered since then.*

I was also feeling spiritually lethargic:

> *in desperation as much as anything, I've decided to fast to recover my spiritual sensitivity and therefore to hear what God is saying to me.*

I used Richard Foster's *A Celebration of Discipline* as my guide. The need to have a sense of God's direction was particularly important to me because I was still missing Calvary and was becoming increasingly frustrated with the leadership of the Cowerbridge congregation and not being able to use my gifts.

But my time of fasting didn't help, and I was becoming increasingly angry and frustrated with the deficiencies of the Cowerbridge congregation. What I didn't fully appreciate then was that Cowerbridge was a mission congregation with none of the advantages of an established church like Calvary. My expectations and needs were never going to be met by such a small pioneering group. I wanted to move, but again felt constrained by Else's friendship with Steve and Jill, and I had no clear sense of where we would move to in any case. It was only a matter of time until things came to a head.

But in the meantime, we tested out possible openings for us as a couple with the Nazareth Hospital in Israel, the location of Else's very enjoyable All Nations placement three years earlier. The chaplain and medical staff of the hospital were helpfully straightforward that while there was an opening for Else, they had no need for an HR professional. I was very happy with that, having absolutely no desire at all to live and work among Arabs. So that was clear enough. But where did that leave us? The answer came soon after. But I didn't recognise it as such.

Towards the end of our trip to Israel a much older English couple in Jerusalem kindly accommodated us in their apartment. Henry and Ruth Backhouse were originally from Cambridge but had lived in Jerusalem for several years where Henry worked as an orthopaedic surgeon. By the time we met them I was thoroughly confused and exasperated by the lack of clear guidance. The 'door' in Israel was closed. 'So what next?' I asked Henry, searching his eyes for some recognition of my anguish and waiting expectantly for a pearl of great wisdom based on his considerable Christian experience. When it came, I didn't recognise it for the wisdom it was: 'Just praise God that he *is* leading you,' he calmly advised as he placed his hand reassuringly on my shoulder. I remember my incredulous internal response: 'That's a fat lot of good! I need to know what, where and when!' But then Henry knew that's what I wanted because I'd already told him.

Thankfully, I got over that initial disappointment and eventually acknowledged Henry's wisdom because in our Pentecost 1990 newsletter a few weeks later we wrote, *the future is still unclear, but we are confident that he is leading us.*

I was soon unemployed again. The Senior Personnel Officer role was maternity cover only. Trevor had encouraged me to apply for a permanent middle management HR vacancy, reporting to him, but I felt I didn't have the required experience. In retrospect, I probably would have been appointed, which would have helped us financially and me psychologically. But at that time I felt it was more important to look for a full-time role in Christian ministry rather than to build an HR career. Yet things just seemed to go from bad to worse. For one thing, Else had health problems which, much to my disappointment, meant that we needed to stay in the UK for a further two to three years. And in May 1990, George, who was Steve's boss at Cowerbridge, intervened to deal with the tensions between me and Steve. I didn't know it at the time, but I was to learn three very important lessons that have stayed with me to this day. I remain very grateful to George and to Steve for that.

I was ready for the meeting with George and had marshalled my facts to support my criticisms of Steve's leadership. George met with us both together and then with each of us alone. When he met with me, he didn't attempt to refute my criticisms but instead asked me to reflect on where I might have failed to maintain the relationship and to be more supportive of Steve. This got me thinking, and I realised that I could indeed have done more. This put me in the right frame of mind to learn George's three lessons. Lesson one: 'You have no right to be angry,' to which I immediately responded, 'I'm not angry!' His simple reply was, 'Yes, you are.' At which point I admitted inwardly to myself, 'He's right.' He took my silence to mean that I agreed and moved onto lesson number two: 'You have no right to carry your hurts.' Well, I knew that I was hurt by this whole sorry saga, so I didn't bother disagreeing. Tacit agreement. Lesson three: 'You have no right to write off another person's ministry.' I attempted to disagree, but he calmly explained that however justified my criticisms were and whatever shortcomings Steve had displayed, it was not my place to judge him, let alone write him off as a leader. Again, I realised that he was right. My anger, pain and judgementalism had blinded me, and I had failed to be as supportive and gracious as I should have been.

I agreed to write a letter of apology to Steve but was not prepared to continue at Cowerbridge. George asked me to reconsider but I could see no future for me there, and therefore none for *us*. George then expressed the hope that we would stay within Ichthus, and I agreed, although I would be very careful about which congregation we joined.

I came away feeling chastised but relieved that I could now leave Cowerbridge. I knew Else would be saddened, but I had shared my struggles with her, and at least it was clear to Steve and Jill that she was not unhappy with Steve's leadership. This was probably the lowest point during our association with Ichthus. We were also experiencing difficulties as newly-weds. But God was at work.

A few months into married life, we both realised that we needed help with our own personal issues. Adjusting to married life is hard enough, and although finding our own place to live helped we keenly felt the need for help. The problem was that we couldn't identify anyone who (1) knew how to help us *and* (2) we trusted to keep our issues confidential. Over dinner one evening we spoke to Jenny, a member of the Cowerbridge congregation, and she told us of a ministry that had completely transformed her father. It was called Wholeness Through Christ (WTC), and the more she told us about it, the more it appealed to us. So that April we wrote to Rev. Trevor Blackshawe at WTC, and with George's support were interviewed in nearby Bermondsey by Rev. Jolyon Bradshaw. He accepted us for our first 'Prayer School' which was to take place in Chislehurst, Kent, from 1st to 5th October that year.

I needed all the help I could get because I was floundering badly: *where has God been in all of this? . . . No job, and clear direction, leaving Cowerbridge congregation, more changes in the offing . . .* Once again, I was wondering about my view of God and how he works. The Cowerbridge crisis indicated that I had been blind to some important personal shortcomings, so I decided I needed to go back to basics and ask the fundamental question: 'Who are you, God?' I returned to J.I. Packer's *Knowing God* and to Eddie Askew's meditations and prayers in his booklet, *A Silence and a Shouting*.

Hopefully as I draw near to God, he will draw near to me, and my self-deception and failure will be dealt with as it should be by the God of love.

I knew I was really struggling. God had indicated that I wouldn't like the move to London, and that was certainly true. But if it was also supposed to be doing me good, it was happening at a painfully slow pace. I needed help and so in late June I went on retreat for three nights to the Anglican Sisters of Bethany in Hindhead, Surrey. I would take Packer and Askew with me, together with my All Nations notes on the topics of guilt, expressing negative emotions, anxiety and anger. My stated aims for the retreat were to strengthen my perseverance and patience, find new ways to enjoy God and rekindle my vision for Muslims.

Chapter 29

The Spirt of Adoption

What I quickly realised was that I was still battling my old enemy, legalism. There seemed to be very little love, mercy and forgiveness in the God I served, so I took Mark 12:28-34 as my text on which to meditate during the retreat. This was an acknowledgement that love really was at the heart of the greatest commandment. At the same time, I set myself to review my experience of Cowerbridge and the lessons learned. It could all have become unhelpfully introspective:

> *I feel like a fraud: God, you forgave me last time and I said I'd try my best! But my best wasn't good enough – it ended in failure! And so the jaw on the floor, the forlorn expression, the feet dragging behind – the reluctant walk back to ask for yet more forgiveness, more mercy, more, more, more! What view of God do I have? . . . Self-forgiveness . . . That's something I need to work at! Lord, please help me while I'm here at Hindhead. Thank you.*

It was a heartfelt and desperate prayer, and the Lord began to answer it through an author who became my main spiritual guide. It was at Hindhead that I first discovered William Temple's *Readings in St John's Gospel*. His commentary on John 8:31-32 emphasises the importance of moving from a Pharisaic reliance on propositional truth alone, which only serves to make us Orthodox believers, to belief in and trust in Christ, which converts us into real Christians. He says:

'When a man is both orthodox and self-assertive, – believing the gospel but not believing *in* it, he is not recognising and making acquaintance with the truth. He is probably quite unconscious that he is in any bondage.'[6]

In reading these words I recognised that during my All Nations studies I'd fallen into the trap of pursuing theological and propositional orthodoxy at the expense of knowing God personally. Temple continues:

'Now, the spirit of legalistic Judaism was precisely the "spirit of bondage" – the spirit in which a man does what is commanded and avoids what is forbidden, hoping for reward and fearing punishment. But the spirit of Sonship . . . is that which prompts us to . . . do at all times what is pleasing to our Father, not for reward or avoidance of punishment, but for love of him.'[7]

Commenting on this in my diary, I realised that I had completely failed to *recognise that the Father is looking for an obedience that flows out of my love for him as a son, rather than that which flows out of my fear of him as a slave would fear his master.*

I continued to meditate and to reflect on Temple's comments during the following enforced months of unemployment. However, I also continued to struggle, and in a diary entry entitled *Struggling* my exasperation shows:

Lord, how about a loud direction to get this devastated soul back into the swing? To which the immediate answer was Psalm 27:14, '*Wait* for the LORD, *be strong* and *take heart* and *wait* for the LORD' (my emphases at the time I wrote those words). This, my diary tells me, *went straight to my heart.*

My next diary entry in September, entitled *Moral Attractiveness*, refers to Temple's comments on The Good Shepherd. He says that the English translation 'Good' should be taken to mean moral attractiveness and not moral austerity: 'It is possible to be morally upright repulsively!'[8] I clearly felt that this was yet another lesson I needed to learn.

Here was the problem: I could see where I was going wrong and what a much more personal and gospel-centred relationship with God should look like. I just didn't know how to get there or who would be able to help me on my journey. Thankfully, I had to wait less than a month for God's provision.

Chapter 30

Wholeness Through Christ

The transformative effects of the WTC prayer ministry are so amazing that it is difficult to know where to begin. The first thing I noticed soon after arriving at Chislehurst for our first prayer school that October was that although the WTC approach included subjects taught as part of the All Nations PCC lectures – sin, guilt, rejection, etc. – the main emphasis was on prayer *ministry* for individuals. The strengths of the PCC lectures were their biblical basis and psychological insights. The strengths of the WTC approach were a complementary biblical paradigm describing the four main areas of human brokenness and, most important of all, a hands-on model of ministry leading to profoundly changed lives. In addition, the ministry sessions were led by people with a track record of being used by God and who were unknown to us. They therefore met our deep needs for competence and confidentiality. We felt we were in very safe hands. That was vital because the Lord was wanting to do a lot of deep work in both of us. The team took the Spirit-led nature of this ministry very seriously. There was no question of us having to do or say anything we didn't want to, and it was so encouraging to know that a team of intercessors prayed before, during and after the prayer school itself. There was teaching, but we were encouraged not to take many notes but instead to simply listen to what the Lord was saying, and then bring that with us to our individual prayer ministry appointments (PMAs).

I approached my PMA feeling both anxious and expectant. I could see that the WTC team members themselves had an attractive lightness of spirit and joy in their lives, and their personal testimonies gave me hope that the Lord could change me too. I was also impressed that each PMA was scheduled to take between three to four hours. To have the undivided attention of three people for this length of time was a great gift: it was a strong signal that those ministering were in no hurry, would go at my pace and take as long as I needed. I had been prayed for in other Christian contexts, but only for a few minutes and with limited results. This was clearly something completely different, and I assumed that the ministry would be wide-ranging and thorough. This was apparent in the introductory teaching sessions which described the brokenness of each person in terms of sin, wounds, bondages (damaged relationships) and oppressing spirits, as well as the oft-forgotten impact of negative inherited roots. I realised right from the start that my PMA would cover all of those areas. And so it proved.

The depth and breadth of the ministry I received is indicated by the section of the personal worksheet I used entitled 'What God Has Done For Me'. This recorded the specific issues covered during my PMA. One subheading is labelled 'Sin', and I listed seven issues here, including a death wish and fear of failure and rejection. Under the 'Bondage' heading there are nine issues, and five under the 'Oppressing Spirits' category including – unsurprisingly

– my grandmother's occult involvement. Last but not least there are four listed under 'Wounds'. Twenty-five in total!

But most importantly of all, I was confident that these issues had truly been dealt with under the leading of the Holy Spirit. I had beforehand some idea of my 'issues', but the sheer breadth and depth of the ministry and its personal relevance was something completely new. Participants usually attend two further prayer schools for reinforcement and further help, but in my case this first PMA was unquestionably a major turning point, and for Else too. The results are best summed up in the words I wrote in bold capitals at the bottom of my personal worksheet:

I WILL LIVE MY LIFE AS A PERSON WHO IS OF VALUE AND IMPORTANCE TO GOD.

This fundamental shift is reflected in the change of tone in my diary entries from October 1990 onwards. Yes, I still had to consolidate what I had received and to 'walk it out' in my daily life, but my eyes had been opened to a completely new and powerful way of receiving the all-embracing and unfathomable love of God. I was able to trust God in new ways, with a real hope that he wasn't indifferent to my concerns after all.

Because of the impact of this ministry on me personally, and its potential for others dealing with similar issues, I feel that it requires further elaboration. A personal example will perhaps elucidate.

While I was living at the children's home I yearned to be reunited with my parents and particularly with my mother. That yearning was never satisfied. The pain of the separation from my parents fuelled my angry outbursts and produced in me a deep sense of helplessness. My parents' failure deprived me of their love, and despite the wonderful love and care I received from others, this deprivation wounded me, leaving me feeling deeply rejected, unloved, insignificant and unimportant. Most of all, I felt insecure and very lonely, and completely unable to change my circumstances.

The Lord showed me during the PMA that although I had verbally forgiven my parents and particularly my mother for their failings, the raw wound was still unhealed, meaning that I continued to experience intense pain and outbursts of anger. I felt that my attempts at forgiveness were like boomerangs that I 'threw' as far as I could, and this gave some relief for a time but then sooner or later the 'boomerang' would make an unwelcome return in the form of the same painful feelings. I needed something more than to express words of forgiveness; I needed the healing power of the Holy Spirit.

As an aside, this highlights what I believe to be the fundamental weakness of some well-meaning approaches to this kind of pastoral problem. There is a belief that if we forgive others, then healing will necessarily follow. The subject is persuaded to speak out their forgiveness of the offender to the Lord, and then to receive forgiveness themselves. This is supposed to free them from the sin of withholding forgiveness and its consequences. This is fine as far as it goes. But it does not go nearly far enough when the person sinned against has been as deeply wounded as I was. There is a real need for healing of the wound which is the source of so much pain. This is particularly relevant to those who have been wounded as children and still carry those wounds into adulthood. To put it another way: speaking forgiveness in cases like mine is a necessary but not a sufficient condition for *deep healing* to take place.

We are created to be in relationship with others and so separation is our most basic pain. In my case, I had only dealt with the surface level of separation from my parents because that is all I knew. What I had never really faced was just how deep that wound was. I had always been wary of digging too deep and felt I either had to live with my pain or that time would heal. I had also never felt safe enough or courageous enough to face that very deep and threatening pain. Who knew how destructive it might be if I tried to face it? What if I fell apart or had a mental breakdown of some kind? Unless I could find someone I could really trust to help me, I just didn't feel safe enough to go there.

Consequently, I pushed the pain down to the point where I could no longer give it a name or recognise its role in fuelling my periodic episodes of unexplained anger. The important point is that I was not fundamentally an angry man, but rather a man in deep pain. And I would have stayed that way if I had never felt safe enough to recognise that suppressed pain, to name it, and to give it to God and then receive his deep healing. Up until then I remained confused and often asked myself, 'Why do I still feel that this issue is unresolved and "alive"? Why am I still not at peace about this issue?' That is precisely how I had felt before my first PMA, but at that time the Lord graciously gave me real insight and showed me, with the help of others, the way through it to healing and freedom.

Not that this was the end of my healing journey. It wasn't. At subsequent prayer schools my eyes were opened to the destructive yet often unseen power of reactive sins, unhealthy relationships and negative self-talk. I realised that these were real for me, and additional barriers to my growth as a Christian. And there was a further positive outcome: because WTC places great importance on training others for this ministry, I was progressively encouraged under the direction of those with greater experience to use these insights to minister to others. As I received healing, the Lord was able to use me as a channel of healing.

WTC was an amazing blessing for both of us, but I was still having to deal with the challenge of nine months' unemployment and all the pressures that put on our finances and on our new life together.

However, my diary entries now suggest that I was at last coming to terms with the fact that God wasn't quite as anxious as I was to get me into full-time Christian service. I still entertained various thoughts about returning to Cardiff, serving in the East End of London or overseas, and buying a house, etc., but I now committed myself to taking *each day, one day – not two days – at a time*. The next entry, just 15 days later, is entitled *Realignment* and it confirms my acceptance of God's will as it was rather than trying to determine matters largely on my own terms. In that entry I make four requests or commitments:

1. that the Lord rekindle in me a desire to work overseas with Muslims if that were his will for us;

2. that I was willing to stay in London if Else or I sensed that the new full-time position at Calvary about to be advertised was not right;

3. that the Lord would help me to be content in my HR work, *rather than a Stoic who perseveres with grimness*;

4. and that I would be able *to find my true security in You, and to love and obey You no matter what the future holds.*

The extremely valuable lessons I learnt through WTC are best summed up by something I came across some years later in a passage from Sister Kirsty's *The Choice*. Quoting the Catholic monk Michel Quoist, Sister Kirsty wrote:

'It is not the place where you are that is the important thing. It is the intensity of your presence there. It is not the situation that counts. What counts is that you are fully alive in any situation . . . Looking hard at the place where you are, instead of wanting to work wonders elsewhere.'[9]

Sister Kirsty's book has become one of my favourites – like a trusted spiritual adviser to which I can turn at any time. And during my last morning at the Sisters of Bethany retreat house that summer I acknowledged the understated wisdom of Henry Backhouse's words and had a real sense that everything was going to be alright. I'm sure that the prayers of the Sisters also helped me leave their home with a deep sense of peace, although it took another six months for my mind and will to align with my heart and spirit. But by the end of the year I had evidently arrived at that place of acceptance with our joint newsletter stating that we were exploring Christian ministry options, but *none bear an obvious mark of the Lord's confirmation.*

In December 1990 I received a permanent offer to begin work with Newham Social Services. It was the most junior

HR role I had filled to date, but I knew I had to prove myself at that level if I was to gain promotion. The new job gave structure to my waking hours and protected me from unhelpful introspection. It was also a useful fill-in while I waited to see if Calvary advertised a planned full-time ministry position. (Which never materialised.)

All in all, the New Year was looking quite a bit rosier than the old, and things were at long last looking up. We had also settled into a new congregation in Dulwich which felt more grounded to us, being full of experienced and very capable Christians. So we looked forward to the new year with some optimism.

Chapter 31

Walter

The job turned out to be a humbling experience. And there were still times when I felt impatient with God's apparent lack of guidance. However, I regularly reminded myself of his unconditional love and his acceptance of me despite my weaknesses, and so I was able to loosen my grip on the need to perform or achieve in order to gain his acceptance or to feel good about myself. 'Walking out my healing' was gradually paying off.

In the worst moments, I wondered if I was simply incapable of discerning God's guidance, but at other times, and especially when meditating on John 16:12-15, I realised that I simply might not be able to *bear* what he might say. Maybe his *silence* might in fact be in my best interests as my mid-January diary entry indicates: *these past years* **haven't** *been missed opportunities, they are preparing you for what's to come!* I realised that in showing me his unconditional acceptance, God was gently encouraging me to own up to *even the bits you hide from yourself,* and to stand against the dominant cultural expectation of 'got-it-togetherness'.

In April 1991, I again went on retreat to the Sisters of Bethany. On this occasion to their Winchester community, during which Stuart Blanch's *Encounters with Jesus* spoke powerfully to me about the illusion of being 'good enough' in order to be used by God. Rather like Bonhoeffer before him, Blanch concluded that the 12 disciples who were later to become apostles had very little to commend them humanly speaking and were far from perfect or particularly competent. It was the fact that the Lord called them and that they obeyed that call that qualified them for the Lord's work. Perhaps there was some hope for me after all.

I also continued to reflect on the WTC insights about self-forgiveness and made a commitment to come to terms with the most serious besetting sins in my life at future prayer schools. It was thus clear to me that the reason there was still *no direction on our future* was that *God is taking more things into consideration than I am aware of.* The Winchester retreat gave him the opportunity to teach me that ministry isn't about performance and success or failure: *In your ministry, be fired by passion, have compassion and begin and finish with mercy for the needy.* With that kind of emphasis, 'failure' is not remotely possible.

And later that year I saw this modelled so well in the lives of Andrew and Mary Matthew. Andrew had been a curate at Else's church in Harwell when Else was a teenager. They were a truly inspirational couple leading a growing Anglican church in the Cornish town of St Austell. When Else introduced them to me I was surprised to discover that they already knew my mother. They had taken an interest in her when she moved nearby before I ever met them, at a time when her health was again very precarious. This was an extraordinary 'coincidence'. But here they were:

Beavering away and enjoying the blessing of their labours – totally devoted to your cause. Their motto seems to be 'forgetting what is behind me, I press on . . .' They have no worldly possessions as such, but their presence points me to their real goal – the treasures of heaven. How I wish, Lord, that I could be so single-minded.

Their example led me to wonder about church-based pastoral ministry. But I still didn't trust my own judgement enough and felt that I might simply be serving my own cause. In any case I was learning to hold such things much more lightly as I worked with the Lord on my own issues.

One of these issues was learning to take the initiative and to face life head-on rather than to expect things to somehow resolve themselves. And I needed to face a potentially very difficult issue head-on. I needed to meet my father. For the first time. Face-to-face. Man-to-man.

One thing that would help to make the meeting easier was that we would be able to stay with Else's Swiss aunt, Doris. Amazingly, she lived within just a few minutes' drive of Walter's residence, in the same part of the canton of Zurich. It couldn't have been more convenient even if someone had planned it.

The meeting would also be easier because we had been corresponding intermittently since I was 19 years old. The correspondence had always avoided sensitive issues, so I never asked about his wife and son, and he never asked about my mother's well-being. I sensed that he would rather write about safer topics such as his work, his hobbies (fishing and local environmental issues) and his holidays.

Interestingly, he had often visited Northern Ireland but had never taken the opportunity to meet me in England. His latest letter in July had been written in a similar vein. No, if we were to meaningfully engage with these issues, then we would have to meet on his home territory, in Switzerland, at a venue of his choosing and with Else present.

Such a meeting was of course fraught with many potential difficulties and damaging outcomes, for both of us. After all, what *are* you going to say to a son who hasn't seen you for 30 years and to whom you are a virtual stranger? Not only that, how are you going to explain your complete absence and silence during all those years when he was languishing in a children's home, knowing that his mother was incapable of carrying out her maternal duties? Furthermore, how are you going to explain why you reneged on your commitments to pay specified amounts into his trust fund which you yourself set up with his mother when he was a baby? How, how, how? This list of potential questions is only matched by the complexity of potential 'Why?' questions your son could ask of you. These would be the 'Why?' equivalents of the 'How?' questions, but also 'how?' questions in their own right. 'How do I relate to this person who is my biological father, but has not functioned as my father?' This was a real question for me, because the fifth of the Ten Commandments says: 'Honour your father and your mother.'[10] It was difficult enough to apply that to my biological mother, given her serious mental health issues and her inability to mother me. If parenthood is more than genetic relatedness (which it is), then what is that 'more'? The biblical concept of adoption points to some answers, and it is of course one of the most powerful metaphors describing the relationship between Christians and the God who – as the Lord's prayer states – is our heavenly Father.[11]

This concept of God as Father and the church as the family of God is also helpful in terms of identity. When we have questions about who we are, the answer usually includes references to our parents. Again, I recall the times when as a child I used to try to imagine what my father was like. It was a fruitless exercise, often ending in a hopelessly idealised man combining the best features of the superheroes Thor and Superman!

It is very likely that he didn't know what he was going to do or say until we actually met face-to-face: that would be the point when he would decide what approach to take. He didn't have long to wait after his letter of July, because in the first week of September 1991 we finally met.

Chapter 32

No Regrets?

The afternoon started well. The weather was sunny and warm, white clouds adorned the blue sky and the pleasant breeze cooled us as we sat on the veranda of the rather expensive restaurant overlooking the lakeside town of Rapperswil. The cuisine was of a high standard and Walter happily paid the bill. After all, he displayed the trappings of someone doing very well for himself: a gold Rolex watch on the wrist of a tanned if somewhat overindulged body; expensive clothes, stylish shoes and designer shades. He seemed to be at ease as he relaxed in his armchair, surrounded by all that was familiar to him. The small talk had been relaxed and good-natured. But as we settled down to our coffees we finally came to the expected pregnant pause in the conversation. He broached the subject first: 'David, I have done nothing in my life that I regret.' I hadn't expected such a complete denial of his responsibility for his actions. After all, wasn't this the man who had refused to marry my mother and provide the right kind of start for me in a stable two-parent family? And who was it who had chosen not to visit, phone or write to me during my time in care? The impact on me had been devastating, and he probably knew that. But he nevertheless chose denial over acknowledgement. Perhaps it was just too much for him to admit.

What he didn't know was that my response was going to be the same whatever he said. So I said it anyway: 'I forgive you.' I could see that this was unexpected and left him slightly bewildered as if to say, 'Where did that come from?' So I elaborated: 'The reason I can forgive you, Walter, is because I know what it is to be forgiven. Because Jesus Christ has forgiven me.' I could see that he was still trying to make sense of this. Perhaps he had been expecting a physically or verbally aggressive response. And what had religion got to do with this in any case? Either way, he sat there with his mouth slightly open saying nothing. So I decided to explain the gospel.

We have all failed and we have all made mistakes. We all know that. The question is: 'What do we do with that uncomfortable fact?' One option is to deny this or play down its significance. The Christian answer is that when we acknowledge our failings, and sincerely commit to doing things God's way that he forgives us and gives us a new identity and ability to live differently. However, the bad news is that forgiveness comes at a price and we, as flawed human beings, are unable to pay that price. But the good news is that Jesus Christ, the perfect human being, paid that price on our behalf as he gave his life for each one of us. The staggering truth is that he did that willingly and in so doing offers a new start for all of us. That is why the cross of Christ is the central symbol of Christianity. It shows us the sacrificial love of the Son of God but it also tells us that although our forgiveness is free to us, God in Christ paid a real price on our behalf.

It was because I understood that God had freely forgiven me that I was able to freely forgive Walter. Because this had profoundly changed me, I knew how much Walter needed my forgiveness and, ultimately, God's forgiveness. It really was as simple and as straightforward as that.

That's why, for my part, I demanded nothing of him and needed nothing from him. It would have been nice to have received an apology, but I hadn't been counting on it. I half-expected that he would need time to lower his defences and admit to himself that he owed me that. And I was right. Eight years later we were visiting Else's aunt Doris and were saying our farewells on the way to Zurich airport. Walter was present too, and I noticed him on his own standing slightly at a distance, looking uneasy and even vulnerable. He seemed very reluctant to say goodbye – almost sorrowful – so I instinctively walked towards him and without really thinking about it reached out to embrace him. He immediately responded in the same way. As we embraced, he quietly said, 'I've been wanting to do this for such a long time, David!' With tears in his eyes he continued, 'I often wondered how you were doing growing up in the children's home all alone.' I looked at him with a smile of thanks and a nod of appreciation.

No regrets? It is one thing to *say* 'I forgive you', and quite often that is all that is necessary to mend the damaged relationship. But my invitation to embrace showed Walter that I really meant what I said. And embracing him and hearing his heartfelt regret in person was important for me too. After our first meeting eight years earlier I had written in my diary that he was *So nice, gentle, open, generous, kind, full of humour and experience.* But I also went on to say, *I want him to take responsibility, but he hasn't done that completely yet . . . I don't think he can face me on his own yet.*

Sometimes people just need time to process their thoughts and feelings and then to feel safe enough to express their sorrow without fear of retaliation or revenge. And that often means that those of us who have suffered need to be ready to move towards them in their vulnerability with a love and acceptance beyond any words we may say.

There was, of course, no way that we could ever recover the lost years. Our relationship would never be magically transformed into some kind of renewed father-son relationship. And we would never be able to put the past behind us as if it had never happened or didn't matter. But our future relationship could still be worthwhile, and I drew comfort from two passages in the Bible in which God addresses the issue of restitution. And I am particularly indebted to Dr Marion Ashton (visiting PCC lecturer at All Nations) for these insights. The first is found in Numbers chapter 5,[12] in which the person who has robbed another must make amends by adding a fifth to what they give back as restitution. In this way, the old covenant principle of restitution was established, and it is expressed in new covenant terms in Hebrews chapter 9. Here the writer explains how the old covenant (or arrangements) for forgiveness are 'external regulations applying until the time of the new order'.[13] He then goes on to say that the new order is inaugurated by Christ, the perfect high priest and the perfect sacrifice, who perfectly fulfils this principle of restitution, declaring: 'How much more, then, will the blood of Christ, who through the eternal Spirit offered himself unblemished to God, cleanse our consciences from acts that lead to death, so that we may serve the living God!'[14] (my emphasis).

In other words, the restitution made by Christ is perfect and eternal. Under the old arrangement, the offender added a fifth to that which they had taken from the other person, and in this way the loss was restored, and the matter settled. Under the new arrangement, not only does Christ redeem (pay back) what was lost, but he pays it back plus, plus!

So, however much others have failed us we can be sure that God has in some way made *ultimate* provision for that failure and that he will one day make that clear to us. But God also invites us to enter into whatever restitution is offered to us *now*. It is not always possible or wise to re-engage with those who have hurt us. But I sensed that Walter wanted to establish a qualitatively better relationship with me that reflected that principle of restitution and so I tried in my own way to apply that principle to my relationship with him.

Much of what this means is beyond our understanding and ultimately a divine mystery. But for Walter and me, forgiveness made it possible for us to have a relationship that though different was still rewarding. We learnt to appreciate each other for who we were, and one of the ways we did this was by discussing things that were important to us. For me, this was my faith; for him it was the human potential movement and local environmental issues.

On one memorable occasion when I visited him – memorable because it was the last time I would see him alive – he mentioned a couple who had recently become Christians and had talked to him enthusiastically about their new-found faith. His response to me was, 'It just seems too good to be true!' I explained that from his humanistic perspective it *was* too good to be true. How could the offer of new life be free? But it is. The sticking point for Walter, as it is for many people, is the issue of trust. Sometime before this, he had told me that he had been through a messy divorce and that his relationship with another woman was coming to an end. With this in mind, I said to him, 'People may let you down, Walter. Your wife may let you down, your parents may let you down, your children and friends may let you down and you may even let yourself down. But Jesus will *never* let you down.' With tears in his eyes he replied, 'Fine words, David. Fine words,' as if to say, 'If only I could believe that like you do.' I don't know what, if anything, passed between him and the Lord during his final days – including three days in a coma – before the cancer finally took him. Of course, I would like to think that he remembered my words and, however falteringly, chose to believe that they were true, that the free gift was still on offer, and that he put his trust in the love and mercy of God.

He wasn't a bad man. In fact, as I have already indicated, my initial impression of him was positive. He, like all of us, had his failings, and sensed that there was more to life. He was genuinely looking for spiritual truth and reality, although he had been very clearly put off Christianity by his wife's version of Roman Catholicism and had reached a dead-end with the human potential movement. He once asked me if I forced people to convert to Christianity, to which I replied, 'No, I act more like a member of an introductions agency!' – an answer which seemed to please him. But again, I do not know if Walter finally put his trust in Jesus. That is between him and the Lord.

He died in 2003, and in one of his last letters to me he wrote for the first time, 'I love you.' This and the terms of his will reflected how far we had come in developing a relationship of mutual respect and affection. The bulk of the estate would go to Andy, his son by his Spanish wife, Pepita. That was right and proper. But to my surprise I was to receive half of his cash savings, with the other half going to Andy. It was a five-figure sum, not much by modern standards. But according to Andy it was something Walter wanted me to have, and Andy clearly wanted to see his father's wishes honoured. So I accepted the gift on that basis. To me this change to his will was significant in two ways. First, it was his attempt at restitution, at least symbolically, for the failure to pay what he had agreed into my trust fund. Second, it was his way, even in death, of acknowledging me as his son. And years later, I learned something that reinforced that conclusion. This was made possible because at that time the Homes informed me that due to changes in privacy laws, I could now access my childcare records. These records contained correspondence between Walter and the Homes, and included a copy of a letter that Walter wrote seven months after my mother's breakdown having rejected the Addison's suggestion in June 1965 that he take care of me because of my mother's inability to do so. Written to my *mother* from Monte Carlo and dated 11th February 1966 when I was only six years old, part of it reads:

> If you are disturbed as to David's future, so am I. I think that adoption would definitely be wrong, and it would be unjust to David. From your letter I gather that though you might move to Kent, David would still be a problem to you. I have talked this over with my

wife and we thought that we should take care of him if that is all right with you. When I left Switzerland, I left a great deal of financial headaches behind which are going to be a heavy burden for the next two years. However, we think we could manage to have him here, and we would try hard to give him both a good home and a better future. If you would agree to this, I believe this would be a fair arrangement, and it is important for him – the sooner the better – to have a permanent home and guidance. Problems resulting from such a transfer would be certain, but they are minor in view of what may come if he stays at Birchington.

Walter never once mentioned to me that he had made any such offer. I don't know why, but he chose not to. As it turned out, my mother did not relinquish legal custody, meaning that I would stay at the Homes for another 11 years. But without this letter I would have continued to believe that Walter had abdicated *all* responsibility for me. This correspondence was evidence that both he and his wife Pepita were genuinely concerned for my well-being, and that they wanted to ensure that I grew up with a family rather than in an institution, no matter how caring.

And I am grateful that I know that now.

Chapter 33

The Two Mothers

But what of my mother? In a sense, it could be said that I had two 'mothers'.

It was my second WTC prayer school that helped me come to this important insight. I was thankful to be back in a safe place with trusted friends where I could receive help with the next 'layer' of my needs. It has been said that the WTC ministry can be likened to peeling off the layers of an onion, because sometimes there are tears. In my case, the tears were always beneficial and, at this second school, the Lord highlighted the issue of 'institutionalisation'. This has been defined as 'suffering the ill effects of long-term residence in a residential institution'. In my case, the Homes became like a mother to me and, much to my astonishment, I had bonded to it at a very deep level indeed. This 'mother' provided safety, love, food, companionship, security and a sense of significance and worth. Which is why I dreaded the day when I would be forced to leave. Who then would provide for these needs of mine? The Homes had made several attempts to get me adopted, but I had rejected them all. So I now had nowhere to go. No wonder I felt such dread and anxiety at the prospect of leaving.

One of the ways this fear would manifest itself was as follows. Whenever a major sports event such as the Olympics or the football World Cup came around, I would worry about where I would be and what I would be doing at the time of the next such event four years hence. When I was younger, the answer was simple: I would still be at the Homes. But when I reached 14 years of age, I realised that I no longer knew what the answer was. Although this uncertainty spurred me on to do as well as possible at school in the hope that education would provide good prospects beyond the Homes, I still worried deeply about how and if I would survive on my own.

I saw other children leaving to live with parents or other relatives who provided some kind of base and security. But I wouldn't have that option. Others would join the Armed Forces, exchanging one form of institutional care for another, and maybe also seeking some kind of substitute parental figure. But I wasn't at all sure that I wanted several more years of being told what to do and being dependent on yet another institution. In any case, my colour-blindness definitively closed that option for me.

So as the days, weeks, months and years slowly ticked by I found myself becoming more and more anxious about my post-Homes future. That was lessened to some extent when I changed to a better school which would help me progress to A-levels once I left the Homes. But I distinctly remember spending the best part of a sunny spring morning sitting under the pink cherry blossom near John Honey's house and feeling very melancholic indeed as I pondered my future after the Homes. In my mind I rehearsed how I would feel on that day when I would be forced to leave, with no prospect of return. I felt so devastatingly sad. I would lose so many things that I valued, things that defined who I was, and which were essential to my well-being. I would no longer have a place to call home (even if I was somewhat ambivalent about calling the Homes 'home'). I would no longer be able to settle down at night knowing what to expect the following day: a nicely cooked breakfast, companionship, and a familiar routine to the day. The ways in which the Homes met my needs, day in and day out, were endless. And it was all – one dreadful day – going to end in a huge wrench. And, as I have described, it did.

What the second prayer school revealed was that I had indeed bonded in important ways to the Homes like a child bonds to its mother, and my forced departure had created a terribly deep wound. For me, it was more than the psychological concept of 'separation anxiety'. If I was to describe this in my own words, it would be as if conjoined twins were physically ripped apart from each other. It was that kind of deep, indescribable pain which inevitably left a devastating mark on me. Ten years on at the second prayer school, I was still grieving the loss of the Homes and all it meant to me. It was like grieving a death: I still felt *that* much pain. This was exacerbated by not having a natural mother (or father) who could take the place of the Homes.

I had also developed an unhealthy fear of being dependent on others, meaning I had developed an unhelpful independence. I was unable and unwilling to rely on others to meet my needs because of the risk of being hurt again. This was an example of what WTC called a 'reactive sin', and I found this concept incredibly helpful. William Temple had already taught me that the most powerful sins are the ones which we are not even conscious of. But WTC went further, showing me that this invisibility is often accompanied by a kind of spiritual 'knee-jerk' reaction: someone or something triggers intense pain from our unhealed wound, and we spontaneously react to that pain. Rather like a rubber hammer causing a knee-jerk reaction. An example of this might be an overreaction which is clearly disproportionate to the triggering event, such as an innocent remark triggering explosive anger. These insights helped me understand so much of my behaviour and the underlying causes, setting me on the road to healing and renewal.

But my mother never found that road. And perhaps she never could.

She, like Walter, died in her mid-60s. In some ways her experience of institutional care mirrored mine. She lived at the Homes for four years as a child and then at St Augustine's for most of her adult life. During the 1980s large mental health institutions like hers were closed in favour of supervised care in the community. When my mother was discharged from St Augustine's, she decided to move to Cornwall, far away from her painful institutional memories. From then on, she lived in a supported living scheme with Philip, her much younger boyfriend, who was almost a child substitute. Philip also suffered from serious mental health problems, but it was clear that they were very devoted to each other and benefitted from each other's company.

Visiting my mother was difficult for all kinds of reasons. First of all, it was so far away, needing the best part of a day to get there by car. Second, I could never be sure what state of mind she or Philip would be in when I arrived. She always seemed awkward with me – perhaps she sensed my ambivalence about visiting – and would sometimes ask soon after I arrived when I was leaving again. This improved when Else accompanied me: her natural kindness and compassion put my mother at ease, and I could see that she was much more relaxed and natural when Else was present. Perhaps that was because of a feminine connection that was beyond me, but I think it was partly because I triggered conflicting emotions in my mother.

Seeing me brought back some of the most painful years of her life. At that time, I didn't know that Walter and Pepita had offered to raise me as their own son and that my mother had not consented. So perhaps I reminded her that her decision had condemned me to lonely years in care and an uncertain future beyond that. She must have had some idea from her own childhood experiences of how much I would have struggled, and I suspect she probably felt guilty about this.

Towards the end of her life she was confined to her bed, and on one occasion we talked very briefly about my time at Spurgeon's. I tried to reassure her that I had been well looked after, and that if there was anything to forgive, then I forgave her. But even though she seemed able to accept that I held nothing against her, I sensed that she was unable to forgive herself. She seemed to believe that it was right to continue to condemn herself as some kind of penance. She also seemed angry at God for her circumstances and always dismissed my offers to pray for her. Although I felt powerless to help her, I live in hope that when she departed this life the Lord, in his compassion and mercy, embraced her with open arms, lifted forever the burden of her guilt and restored her to her rightful mind. For he has promised that: 'He will wipe every tear from their eyes. There will be no more death or mourning or crying or pain, for the old order of things has passed away.'[15]

I am also grateful that my mother warmed to Else and showed her appreciation from time to time by buying her little presents. The last item she bought was a small vanity set which Else still uses. We both value it, for one thing because it reminds me of my mum – the *real* mum who occasionally emerged from behind the fog of strong medicines and a tortured mind. But also because it provided Else with a glimpse of the woman who gave me life and tried her best despite her own very difficult start in life and her crippling mental health.

On the day of her funeral, just a few of us paid our respects. Mental health has a very powerful isolating effect, and, apart from Philip, my mother had no real friends – and certainly none well enough to attend the service. It is perhaps understandable that people are rather afraid of those who are seriously mentally ill, and uncertain how to interact with them. Even I experienced discomfort and uncertainty about what to do or say when I was visiting her and Philip. The uneasy situation was made even more difficult when my mother seemed not to appreciate the effort I had made to visit. But that was all part of her illness, and I eventually came to accept that.

I also came to accept that although I would have wished it differently, Virginia was indeed my mother. Yes, she failed me (as did Walter), and I had paid a huge price. But they were both young and she had been robbed of a sound mind for most of her adult life.

So I am grateful to both mothers: the mother who gave me life and the 'mother' who kept me safe and cared for me.

Chapter 34

Justice, Forgiveness, Hope ...

When we have been wronged and especially when we feel powerless and in pain, we cry out for justice. But we may never get that 'justice' or even an acknowledgement of wrongdoing. And yet, we deserve to be at peace. We *need* to be at peace. The apostle James tells us that 'mercy triumphs over judgement'[16] and it is that principle that is at the heart of the Christian faith. But does that mean that justice isn't important? And if it is important, then how does justice relate to forgiveness?

No one would pretend that forgiveness is easy. For those of us who have experienced deep pain, forgiveness is often a *process* that runs alongside our healing, and our feelings may well take time to catch up with our expressions of forgiveness. And just because we forgive the other person does not mean that they should not be held accountable in some way. It doesn't. What we can be sure of is that God will ultimately call them to account. But an essential part of forgiveness is the decision to give up any claim to take revenge – however subtle and well-disguised – on those who have deeply hurt us. For the Christian, forgiveness is modelled by Jesus Christ who, even as he was dying, prayed for those who were responsible for crucifying him,

'Father, forgive them, for they do not know what they are doing.'[17]

And it *is* true: those who have hurt us most can never know just how much pain they *have* inflicted because so much of it is hidden from them and they can never fully enter into our experience of it. For many years, I was in deep pain. But my parents could never really comprehend the full consequences of their actions, and it wasn't necessary for them to know all the details because that would not have helped them or me. But before my parents died, I was able to forgive them from my heart. I released them from any claim to justice and asked God to bless them. Partly because it was the right thing to do, but also because I wanted closure. I *needed* closure. And that closure released me from the heavy burden I had been carrying for so many years.

And we ourselves need forgiveness, whether we realise it or not. No, *we* didn't nail Jesus to the cross, but we all know that we have not always loved God or our neighbours as ourselves. And if we are honest we have at times fallen well short of that standard. That means that we are all in some measure deserving of God's judgement. But in the death of Christ, God has provided a way for mercy to triumph over judgement. Christ has willingly taken *our* place in the court of divine judgement and paid the penalty that we should have paid for our wrongdoing. In that sense he is the *ultimate* victim of injustice. But it is as we make the forgiving words of the crucified Christ our own, that we are able to bring those who deserve our judgement to the foot of the cross. To leave them there. And to leave our desire for justice there too. It is as we spend time looking upon the crucified Christ that we are able to offer him the pain of our own hearts. And as he takes our pain deep into himself, we know that justice is being done, that the penalty is paid and we are able to hear the blessed voice saying, 'It is finished!'[18] And so we turn confidently and in faith towards a new beginning with renewed hope.

We may need to repeat this act of forgiveness over time until it becomes real to us. And we may need human help to 'walk it out'. But it is this divine provision that enables us to move on from being defined as victims. We may feel justified in telling others and ourselves that we have a right to withhold forgiveness. After all, 'they did *that* to me, and I have a *right* to be angry, a right to hold on to *my* pain and a *right* to justice!' Not that anyone would want to deny that I *have* suffered and that I *am* unquestionably a victim of injustice. But do I want to remain a victim for the rest of my life, rehearsing the same internal dialogue? Or do I want to find a way to move on from defining myself as a victim? As I said, we may never receive the justice we want. Where does that leave us? Is there another way?

There are many who have walked this path before us. Years later I was present at a public meeting when Father Michael Lapsley talked to the traumatised people of East Timor in the run-up to independence. The Timorese had, over many years, experienced unimaginably great suffering at the hands of the Indonesian military. They told Father Michael that they wanted justice before they could move towards forgiveness and reconciliation. He told them that 'there is a form of justice that stores up problems for the future' and that during the South African apartheid era he received a letter bomb that blew off both his hands and blinded him in one eye. He said that after the bomb he realised that if he was filled with hatred and a desire for revenge he would be a victim forever, like so many before him. But in forgiving, the way opened for him to move from victim to survivor and from survivor to victor.[19] It was this kind of testimony that led to the Timorese establishing their own version of the South African Truth and Reconciliation Commission.[20]

But we can go further. I would like to add with the apostle Paul that we can become *more* than victors, or, in Paul's words, 'more than conquerors'. Referring to the many injustices he had suffered as a follower of Christ, Paul nevertheless concludes, 'In all these things we are *more than conquerors* through him who *loved* us'[21] (my emphasis). Paul experienced the very real pain and humiliation of multiple injustices at the hands of many people 'yet in *all* these things' his personal experience of God's love gave him victory and enabled him to become more than a conqueror. Notice, too, that Paul says '*we* are more than conquerors'. The invitation is extended to each of us. Two thousand years after Paul penned these wonderful words, that same love of Christ set me on the journey from victim to more than a conqueror.

That journey begins for each of us as we choose to put off our old, wounded identity and embrace our true identity 'in Christ'. We choose to live our lives as people who truly are important and valuable to God. We no longer permit the voices of the past to define us, but rather allow God's love to shape us. And as we respond to God's voice our feelings and thoughts begin to change, and we increasingly become the people God always intended us to be. We are also able to discover God's purpose for our lives.[22] And as *we* are transformed we give hope to *others* that there is a way through the pain and injustice and that the future can be so much better than the past.

And we can choose to start that journey right now. After all, God hasn't changed: he loves us now and he loves us always. That was true for me as a despairing 19-year-old on a cold, dark November night many years ago. It is just as true today.

For me. And for you.

Notes

1. Psalm 139:13, 16.

2. Colin Chapman, *The Case for Christianity* (Eerdmans Publishing Co., April 1984).

3. 1 John 4:4.

4. Dietrich Bonhoeffer, *The Cost of Discipleship* (Translation: SCM Press, 1948, 1959, Eleventh Impression 1980), page 49.

5. Matthew 6:21.

6. William Temple, *Readings in St John's Gospel (First and Second Series)* (MacMillan and Co. Limited, St Martin's Street, London, 1947), page 142.

7. *Ibid* page 143.

8. *Ibid* page 166.

9. Sister Kirsty, Community of St Mary the Virgin, *The Choice* (London: Hodder & Stoughton), page 197. Copyright © Sister Kirsty, 1982.

10. Exodus 20:12.

11. Matthew 6:9.

12. Numbers 5:5-10.

13. Hebrews 9:10.

14. Hebrews 9:14.

15. Revelation 21:4.

16. James 2:13.

17. Luke 23:34.

18. John 19:30.

19. https://www.theforgivenessproject.com/stories-library/michael-lapsley/ (accessed 31.03.2022).

20. For a powerful testimony to the power of forgiveness at a national level, see Desmond M. Tutu, *No Future Without Forgiveness* (Random House, 1999).

21. Romans 8:37

22. A good place to start is Rick Warren's book *The Purpose Driven Life* (Grand Rapids, Michigan: Zondervan, 2002). For more details and online resources visit: https://www.purposedriven.com/ (accessed 16.06.22).

Resources

Wholeness Through Christ UK

https://www.wholenessthroughchrist.org/
(accessed 07.07.2022)
Tel: 01324 714 946 or write to: 51 Maddiston Road,
Brightons, Falkirk, FK2 0JR.

With branches in Canada, France, Finland and South Africa.

Other organisations with a similar approach include:

Crowhurst Christian Healing Centre

The Old Rectory,
Crowhurst,
Battle,
East Sussex
TN33 9AD

Phone: 01424 830033
enquiries@crowhursthealing.org.uk
https://www.crowhursthealing.org.uk/
(Accessed 12.08.22)

Ministries of Pastoral Care

https://ministriesofpastoralcare.com/about-us/
(accessed 07.07.2022)
Ministries of Pastoral Care
P.O. Box 60255
Shoreline, Washington 98160, USA.

e-mail: info@ministriesofpastoralcare.com
With ministries in the US, France and Switzerland.

Harnhill Centre of Christian Healing

https://www.harnhillcentre.org.uk/
Tel: 01285 850283 or write to: Harnhill Manor, Harnhill,
Cirencester, GL7 5PX

Journey UK

https://www.journey-uk.org/ *(accessed 07.07.2022)*
P.O. Box 75864, London, SW11 9NL.
email: hello@journey-uk.org or call on 020 7799 2200

Ellel Ministries

https://ellel.uk/about/#about-us-who
Frensham Road, Farnham, GU10 3DL.

Acorn Christian Healing Foundation

https://acornchristian.org/
c/o Westmead House, Westmead, Farnborough, GU14 7LP.

Spurgeon's Children's Charity can be found at: https://spurgeons.org/

A series of memories written by some of those who lived at the Birchington site can be found at: https://spurgeons.org/about-us/our-heritage/

Printed in Great Britain
by Amazon

16712663R00169